relationships

Leader's Guide

Resources by Les and Leslie Parrott

Books

Becoming Soul Mates
Getting Ready for the Wedding
Like a Kiss on the Lips
Love Is
The Marriage Mentor Manual
Questions Couples Ask
Relationships
Relationships Workbook
Saving Your Marriage Before It Starts
Saving Your Marriage Before It Starts Workbook for Men
Saving Your Marriage Before It Starts Workbook for Women

Video Curriculum

Saving Your Marriage Before It Starts
Mentoring Engaged and Newlywed Couples

Audio Pages

Relationships
Saving Your Marriage Before It Starts

Website

www.realrelationships.com

relationships

An Open and Honest Guide to Making Bad Relationships Better and Good Relationships Great

Leader's Guide

Drs. Les and Leslie Parrott
with Sharon E. Lamson

ZondervanPublishingHouse
Grand Rapids, Michigan

A Division of HarperCollins*Publishers*

Relationships Leader's Guide

Requests for information should be addressed to:

ZondervanPublishingHouse
Grand Rapids, Michigan 49530

ISBN 0-310-22473-X

Interior design by Sherri Hoffman

Printed in the United States of America

99 00 01 02 03 04 05 /❖ ML/ 10 9 8 7 6 5 4 3 2 1

contents

introduction

"The LORD God said, 'It is not good for the man to be alone. I will make a helper suitable for him'" (Genesis 2:18).When God said that it wasn't good for man to be alone, he wasn't merely referring to Adam and Eve. God created humankind to need relationships—both with him and with other people.

According to researchers, the single most important ingredient to happiness and even to survival is relationships. Authors and psychologists Drs. Les and Leslie Parrott make this point in their book titled *Relationships*. They recall a radio talk show they cohosted in Chicago. After being barraged by callers who wanted to complain about their relationships, Tom, a desperate college student, called the show. After Tom made a few broken attempts to explain why he called, Les asked him, "So what are you feeling, Tom?"

A long silence was finally broken with the word, "Lonely." Les writes, "Something about this word and the way he said it—his frankness and vulnerability—as well as the follow-up discussion, drastically changed the tone of the remaining minutes of the program. The crusty callers and opinionated commentaries seemed to vanish. One caller after the next echoed Tom's emotion. On this Saturday night, all over the country, if only for a few minutes, faceless people phoned in to share the experience of being alone."

Our need to be touched, to communicate, to be appreciated and valued are universal needs. These needs are divinely created—they are not merely learned. During World War II, orphaned babies developed a mysterious disease the doctors called "marasmus." Despite the attempts to stimulate their interest with brightly colored toys, good food, and warm clothing, the babies' conditions worsened. Some even died.

United Nations doctors were asked to intervene. After studying the situation, a simple prescription was ordered. For ten minutes each hour, all children were to be picked up by a nurse, hugged, kissed, played with, and talked to. With this simple prescription, the little ones brightened, their appetites returned, and they once again played with their toys. Their marasmus was cured.

What these babies were suffering from was loneliness. By being in relationship to a nurse for just ten minutes an hour, they gained weight, brightened, and became healthier.

Is it that simple? Would that straightforward prescription work for those of us who are lonely or who have unhappy relationships? As the Parrotts point out, relationships are complex and often difficult to maintain. Often there is no single remedy to the problems we encounter with the people in our lives—starting with our own families.

Though solutions may often be complicated, there are some fundamental principles that can be applied to any relationship. Learn the basics. Apply them to the relationships you care about most—and expect results.

ABOUT THE AUTHORS

Drs. Les and Leslie Parrott, codirectors of the Center for Relationship Development at Seattle Pacific University (SPU), are the founders of a revolutionary program that deals specifically with relationships. Les Parrott is a professor of clinical psychology and his wife Leslie is a marriage and family therapist—both at SPU.

They are authors or editors of several books that address dating and marriage relationships, including *Saving Your Marriage Before It Starts*, *Becoming Soul Mates*, *The Marriage Mentor Manual*, *Mentoring Engaged and Newlywed Couples* (video curriculum), *Questions Couples Ask*, *Like a Kiss on the Lips*, and *Getting Ready for the Wedding*. In addition, they are nationally sought-after guest speakers, and they have written for a number of magazines. Their work has been featured in *USA Today*, *The New York Times*, and on CNN. Guest appearances on television shows include *Good Morning America* and the *Oprah Winfrey Show*.

A COURSE DESIGNED FOR BUILDING RELATIONSHIPS

Their book, *Relationships*, is the foundation upon which this interactive six-week course is built. The course is designed for anyone who is in relationship with anyone else—friend to friend, spouse to spouse, worker to coworker, parent to child—anyone! Its objective is to help bad relationships become better and to make good relationships great.

Please note that chapters 6, 7, and 8 of the book have not been included as part of the general study, as these chapters deal primarily with dating relationships.

INCLUDED WITH THE KIT

Relationships—by Drs. Les and Leslie Parrott. The latest research on contemporary relationships is woven into strategies and solutions in this easy-to-understand book. Both experience and knowledge have gone into its creation, as well as a sincere, heartfelt desire to mend broken relationships and strengthen healthy ones.

Relationships Leader's Guide—Step by step, this guide will help you successfully lead each of the sessions—even if you've never led a small group before.

Relationships Participant's Guide—While a copy of the Participant's Guide is included within the body of the Leader's Guide, a separate book is also included so you can show your class members what they will be using.

Relationships Video—Video clips featuring Drs. Les and Leslie Parrott will introduce each of the sessions and offer a professional perspective to the topics that will be discussed by your group.

OTHER ITEMS YOU WILL NEED

Video player
Monitor with sound system
Name tags
Bible
Pencils or pens for participants who need them
Whiteboard, chalkboard, or overhead projector with appropriate writing tools

USING THIS LEADER'S GUIDE

The *Relationships* Leader's Guide is designed to be comprehensive yet simple and easy to use. Whether you've led a hundred small groups or are testing the waters with this one, the Leader's Guide will help you be a successful facilitator.

To help you walk through the session, we use several typographical elements to indicate what to do:

1. Text that appears without gray boxes can be read verbatim or at times can be changed to meet your group's situation or your own style. Use your own illustrations to augment what the session is trying to convey. Have fun with it—relax!
2. Words shown in ALL CAPITAL LETTERS are words the participants need to fill in the blanks found on the corresponding page in their Participant's Guide. (Example: Sociologist George Herbert Mead once said, "The SELF can only exist in RELATIONSHIP to other selves.")
3. Directions to the instructor are enclosed in a shaded box. These directions are not meant to be spoken by the instructor.

Before the Session

Prior to class time, the leader should (1) read the provided synopsis of material from the corresponding chapter of the book *Relationships*; (2) view the video clips that will be used in the session; and (3) go through the session in the Leader's Guide, making notes as necessary. To give an overview of the lesson and help with time management, a session sequence is provided for each session. For a more in-depth introduction to the session, the leader is encouraged to read the entire chapter from the book *Relationships*.

Participant's Guide Pages

So the leader will know how the material being presented correlates to what the participants are looking at in their guidebooks, a reduced-size copy of the corresponding page or pages in the Participant's Guide is located on the right-hand page of the Leader's Guide. This eliminates the need to juggle two books. Space is provided for the leader to make notes in preparation for leading the session.

SESSION SEQUENCE

The *Relationships* course is divided into six 50-minute sessions. Each session is divided into the following parts:

Welcome

The leader will begin each class by welcoming the participants.

Opening Prayer

The leader may use the prayer provided, or pray extemporaneously.

Review and Overview

This short segment provides a brief summary of the previous session (with the exception of Session 1) and an overview of the content to be discussed in the current session.

Video

All the sessions have an introductory video clip where the authors talk about the material that will be covered. Each clip will have on-screen instructions as to when to turn off the tape. Some sessions include more than one video clip.

Huddle Time

Each session contains "Huddle Times" when participants will be asked to break into small discussion groups of three or four people. Small groups help facilitate the exchange of ideas in a less threatening atmosphere. Limiting the size of the group to three or four people will enhance the possibility of getting everyone involved.

Conference Call

Often sessions will include a "Conference Call" or two—a chance for participants to learn concepts and exchange ideas in a large-group setting. Sometimes spokespersons from the smaller Huddle Time groups can summarize what their group has discussed so the whole class can benefit from their thoughts.

On Your Own

These exercises are done on an individual basis. They are designed to help participants apply the material to their own life circumstances.

Session Summary

To bring closure to the session, the leader will summarize the session.

Extra-Mile Exercise

At the end of each session, the leader will mention the "Extra-Mile Exercise." These exercises encourage participants to do some reading and thinking outside of the classroom. These extracurricular exercises are strictly optional and will not be discussed during subsequent sessions; however, participants who want to do these exercises are encouraged to share their responses with someone close to them.

Closing Prayer

The leader may use the prayer provided or pray extemporaneously. Leaders may also ask a participant to pray.

A WORD ABOUT GROUP DISCUSSIONS

Groups of any size can present unique challenges to those who facilitate discussion. Because group dynamics vary, there are no specific guidelines that will work as a "magic formula" for each group. But there are some general principles you can apply to help your group run smoothly.

Usually groups consist of some basic types of people—those who like the limelight, the behind-the-scenes people, those who enjoy taking the opposite point of view, and people who never say anything. Each person is important to your group, and each type of personality brings a special flavor to group dynamics—it's all how you, as the leader, apply the right guidance to bring about optimal results.

Those Who Like the Limelight

What group would be complete without those bold, sometimes dramatic individuals who just enjoy spontaneously talking? Often they express strong opinions. Many times, these people have stories to tell that may or may not relate to the topic of discussion. These people are uncomfortable with periods of silence, so they fill it up. Sometimes they do so because they don't want the leader to look bad. There are all kinds of reasons why these people are the first (and often the last) to speak up.

Your group would probably be pretty quiet without these individuals, so you do not want to discourage their participation. Yet, without some controls, they could monopolize the discussion and even get it off track. Below are some points to consider in maximizing the valuable input these people have to offer while, at the same time, minimizing their tendency to take over a discussion:

- Allow the person to speak as long as he stays on the subject. When you perceive that he is rambling or veering off track, interrupt him with something like, "Thank you, John, for some valuable insights, but I think we're getting a little off the subject. Does someone else have something to add to what John has just said?"
- When you ask the group a specific question, try to make eye contact with someone other than the people who tend to speak up frequently. That way you can direct the question to someone specifically.
- If someone repeatedly answers questions or makes remarks, you may have to privately speak to that person. Always affirm her for participating but explain that you are trying to solicit response from people who never talk. Let her know that you expect and are okay with silent spots in the discussion. Ask her to help you generate greater group participation by refraining from answering as many

questions. Also let her know that you will call upon her specifically to respond to certain questions to which you believe she would have good input.

The Behind-the-Scenes People

There are wonderful people who don't like to be on stage but love to be in the hub of backstage activity. Whether it's painting the set, designing the costumes, writing the script, or directing the play, they are in their element as long as they don't have to perform.

This personality reacts the same way in group discussion. They may prod someone else to respond or they may write letters afterward expressing their opinion, but they are extremely uncomfortable speaking in front of a large group of people—and the term "large group" is personally defined. Yet these individuals often have very poignant perspectives and opinions from which the whole group could benefit. Below are a few suggestions on how to best include these people:

- Be observant. Look for people who are avidly taking notes or who make side comments to others around them but who don't speak up in large-group discussion. These are most likely your "backstage" participants.
- When opening the floor for discussion, try to direct a specific question to this person. "Martha, how would you respond to the statement . . ." If Martha gives a short answer or merely shrugs her shoulders, say, "That's okay, Martha. We'll get your input on another topic." If she does share, be sure to thank her and affirm her for her response.
- When breaking the group into small groups, you might ask Martha to facilitate the group's discussion. Ask her to be a spokesperson for the group and to report to the large group on what her group concluded.
- If you know the person well and you see him taking notes or making a side comment, you might make a comment like, "Jack, I just know you have some thoughts on this subject. Come on, won't you share one of them with us?" Try to solicit and encourage. And when he does respond, affirm his response. "Thanks, Jack. That was a very thought-provoking observation. Does anyone else have something to add to what Jack just said?"

Those Who Take the Opposite Point of View

You say the sky is blue; they say the sky is gray. There are individuals who enjoy taking the opposite point of view, splitting hairs over the meaning of words and philosophizing over the meaning of statements. Their ability to examine facts from every conceivable angle is truly remarkable, but—as with our limelight friends—their input must be contained to the subject at hand.

If you have someone who gets hung up on semantics, wants to take issue with the material that is being presented, or becomes argumentative, try one or more of the following remedies:

- Ask the person to summarize what he thinks the author's intent was in writing the material. In other words, guide the participant away from his own pontifications and help him to focus on what the author wanted to convey. You may have to redirect his attention to the author's point of view several times, explaining that for the purposes of this class, you are focusing on the material as it is presented by the author.
- If the problem persists and/or the person becomes negative, you may want to talk to him privately. Take time to listen to his opinion. Find out if the material being presented is offensive to him in some way and, if so, why.
- Affirm her for positive contributions made and insights shared. Know your material well enough to dispel any arguments she may bring up to discredit the material being taught. If she voices an opinion that is contrary to what is being presented, counter with something like, "That's a very interesting point that doesn't quite click with what we're trying to accomplish here. I'd be happy to discuss this with you after class, if you wish, when we can explore it further." Don't feel as if you have to have all the answers. Sometimes, just listening and even offering to do some research can help a negative person warm up a bit and be willing to look at the material from a fresh perspective.

People Who Never Say Anything

In every crowd, there are always those people who never say anything. It's not because they're behind-the-scenes people but because they are shy. This doesn't mean they don't have thoughts or opinions. Instead, for whatever reason, they don't feel secure enough to share their opinions in a large-group setting. There are several things to consider with regard to our quiet friends:

- Not everybody verbally expresses what they believe about a statement or question. Be observant. Watch body language—those physical clues that reveal whether a person is bored, excited, angry, happy, or nervous. Learn to read your audience. This is especially important for people who don't talk during class. By watching for their reaction, you may be able to approach them either before or after class to "check in" and find out on a one-on-one basis how they like the class.
- During small-group time, check to see if they feel freer to speak in a smaller group setting. If not, you may want to ask someone in the group to engage him in conversation on a one-on-one basis regarding the material that was presented. You can suggest they solicit opinions about the video, the exercises, or any of the large- or small-group discussions. Encourage them to steer clear of questions that would require simply a yes or no response.

General Tips

- Before class, practice the questions you will ask. It's often helpful to say them aloud in front of a mirror. Knowing your group, will the questions elicit response? Can you anticipate any challenges from participants? If so, how will you handle them?

- Express yourself with warmth, sincerity, and interest. If you are enthusiastic about the material, chances are your class will be too.
- Reword questions as you deem necessary. The material presented is a guideline for you—use it, augment it, or work with it in a way that maintains the integrity of the session yet addresses the personality of both yourself and the class participants.
- Differences of opinion are okay. If you sense that a difference of opinion is turning negative, you may want to intervene by expressing that for the purposes of these sessions, you're going to stick with what the authors have written.
- People need time to think about statements before they respond. If there is some initial silence, that is okay. Be patient. If the class doesn't begin to respond after 15–20 seconds, try rephrasing the question or statement.
- Along with the questions/statements you will be asking the group to respond to, there will be some possible answers printed in your Leader's Guide. These are merely suggested responses. Participants do not have to say the exact word or phrase in order to "get it right." If participants are getting the right idea, then feel free to move on. If they are stuck for ideas, you may want to present a couple of the suggested responses to get them going. Be a good listener.

Session One

the compulsion for completion

BEFORE YOU LEAD

Synopsis

In the autumn of 1992 we did something unusual. We offered a course at Seattle Pacific University that promised to openly and honestly answer questions about family, friends, dating, and sex. In short, its purpose was to teach the basics of good relationships.

The course was to be an informal group with voluntary attendance; any student could be present or drop out at any time if he or she so desired. We called the class "Relationships."

Since that first autumn, we have lectured on campuses and in churches across the country, teaching the basics of good relationships. And we always begin with the same sentence: If you try to find intimacy with another person before achieving a sense of identity on your own, all your relationships become an attempt to complete yourself.

This single sentence holds the key to finding genuine fulfillment for every relationship. Once the truth of this sentence is understood and internalized, you'll discover the abiding comfort of belonging—to family, friends, the love of your life, and ultimately, God.

All of us have struggled with loneliness. We've all felt detached, unaccepted, separated from the group we'd like to be part of. And when we find ourselves in this empty space, we typically search outside ourselves—often compulsively—for something or someone to fill it. The truth is, the cause of our emptiness is not a case of missing persons in our lives, but a case of incompletion in our soul.

The pioneering sociologist George Herbert Mead was known for saying, "The self can only exist in relationship to other selves." In other words, having a relationship, being a member of a community, helps us discover who we are. If we have not achieved a solid sense of who we are on our own, we are destined to believe one of the two subtle lies guaranteed to sabotage all our relationships: (1) I need this person to be complete, and (2) If this person needs me, I'll be complete.

Too many people attach themselves to another person to obtain approval, affirmation, purpose, safety, and, of course, identity. And when the inevitable disappointment happens, they complain bitterly that this person failed them.

The truth is, self-worth does not come from the mere existence or presence of someone in your life. When you come to a relationship lacking personal self-worth, all you can offer is neediness.

The second relationship lie is just as lethal as the first, but more cruel. The person living this lie appears to be less desperate. They aren't contorting themselves to win the approval of another. Instead, they are seeking someone simply to win. Operating out of the same vacuum of personal identity and self-worth, they want a relationship with someone—anyone—who will build up their weak ego. They aren't interested in commitment, only conquest. And the more conquests, the better.

If it's not already crystal clear, we'll say it plainly: There are no shortcuts to personal growth and wholeness. We know from personal experience and the wisdom of others that people who become whole learn to (1) heal their hurts, (2) remove their masks, (3) sit in the driver's seat, and (4) rely on God.

These four steps will take you farther than you think. The test of your determination, however, will be the first one. It's the toughest.

Heal Your Hurts

Repressed feelings, especially painful ones, have a high rate of resurrection. That's why the place to begin your journey toward wholeness is where it hurts.

For some people, personal hurts run deep; for others they appear to be mere scratches. Whatever your situation, this step toward wholeness is crucial. Be aware, however, that healing your hurts is a process of painful self-exploration. Personal growth almost always is. But no matter how painful the process, it's worth the price.

Take Off Your Masks

Why do all of us hide behind masks? We vacillate between the impulse to reveal ourselves and the impulse to protect ourselves. In a seemingly inexplicable paradox, we long both to be known and to remain hidden.

The primary reason we wear our masks is to guard against rejection. If we wear our masks long enough, we may guard against rejection and we may even be admired, but we'll never be whole. And that means we'll never enjoy true intimacy. Here's the situation. When what you do and what you say do not match the person you are inside—when your deepest identity is not revealed to others—you develop an incongruent or fragmented self. You're consumed with the impression you're making on others. You're always wondering what other people think of you.

Sit in the Driver's Seat

It's so easy to be passive—to move through life simply reacting to outside forces. Like passengers on a bumpy bus ride, we watch the scenery flash by our window as life happens around us.

And when it comes to achieving wholeness, to building a solid sense of identity and self-worth, we want something to happen to us. Like magic, we want to be zapped with insight, with wisdom, or even a mystical experience that will change us. The problem is, you don't catch a sense of self-worth from reading a book or attending a seminar or seeing a therapist. Self-worth comes from hard work. It is earned. You will never achieve it as a mere passenger; you must sit in the driver's seat.

All of your relationships, if they are to be healthy, must be predicated on your having an identity, forging a purpose, having courage, and making commitments to things outside yourself. Once you take an active role in the quality of your own life, other people share in your growth rather than becoming responsible for it.

If you are serious about writing your own destiny, you will need a couple of tools. To begin with, you'll want a personal statement of purpose and a small set of meaningful goals.

Rely on God

The final step toward achieving wholeness is one that many fail to take. They may do everything we have discussed so far in this chapter, but they are not maximizing their potential for healthy relationships until they learn to rely on God—not another person—to meet their ultimate needs.

At the core of each of us is a compulsion for completion so strong that no single human can consistently fulfill it. The heart of the issue here is personal significance. This need is woven into the fabric of our nature, our very being. The desperate need for significance is as real as any physical need we ever experience.

While our earthly relationships will let us down time and time again, a relationship with God can be counted on to genuinely and fully meet our deepest need for significance. Only God can ultimately and consistently love us when we are moody, when we make mistakes, and when we feel rejected and unloved by the person we counted on the most.

Session Sequence (50 minutes total)

Welcome (8 minutes)
Opening Prayer (1 minute)
Overview (1 minute)
Video (3 minutes)
Video (7 minutes)
Conference Call (5 minutes)
Conference Call (5 minutes)

On Your Own (5 minutes)

On Your Own (5 minutes)

Huddle Time (5 minutes)

Session Summary (4 minutes)

Closing Prayer (1 minute)

Please note: The first portion of the video tape is a promotional clip, after which the leader will be prompted to turn off the tape until it is time to show the first video clip for Session 1.

Session One

the compulsion for completion

8 minutes

WELCOME

Call the group together. Welcome the participants to Session 1 of *Relationships*: "The Compulsion for Completion."

Introduce yourself. Tell the group your name and a little bit about yourself. Tell them why you are excited to be leading the course.

Hold up the book *Relationships*. Explain that the course is based on this book. Offer the book for sale or tell participants where they can purchase one.

If the size of your group permits, have the participants introduce themselves and mention one thing they hope to learn in this course. Or ask an ice-breaker question such as, "If you could be one musical instrument, what would it be and why?"

1 minute

OPENING PRAYER

Father, we ask that you open our hearts to the truths found in this course. We thank you for the gift of friendship and for the relationships we each enjoy. As we watch the video and discuss the material, help us to focus on developing healthy relationships with others. In Jesus' name, amen.

1 minute

OVERVIEW

Please turn to page 10 in your Participant's Guide for an overview of today's session.

During this first session together, we are going to investigate our relational readiness, uncover two lies that sabotage relationships, take a look at the masks we wear in various settings and discuss ways to discard the unhealthy ones, and explore four steps we can take toward becoming whole.

Session One

the compulsion for completion

Overview

In this session you will

- investigate your relational readiness.
- uncover two lies that sabotage relationships.
- take a look at the masks you wear in various settings and discuss ways to discard the unhealthy ones.
- explore four steps you can take toward becoming whole.

planning notes

3 minutes

VIDEO: The Longing for Belonging

In the introductory video segment, "The Longing for Belonging," we'll meet the program hosts and Drs. Les and Leslie Parrott. We'll see the importance of relationships in our lives and preview the six sessions that will follow.

Start the video; turn it off at the prompt.

7 minutes

VIDEO: The Compulsion for Completion

Turn to page 11 in your Participant's Guide, where you will find space to take notes on the next video segment, "The Compulsion for Completion." In this video, we'll see the importance of personal wholeness and the two lies people often tell themselves that get in the way of wholeness. We'll meet Anne, who seems to feel she needs someone else to make her more whole. And Les and Leslie will go over the four components necessary to becoming whole on our own.

Start the video; turn it off at the prompt.

Now that we've had a chance to watch the video segment, let's review the material. Do you think Anne's attitude is healthy? Could she be showing the compulsion for completion?

5 minutes

CONFERENCE CALL: Two Lies That Sabotage Relationships

Please turn to page 12 in your Participant's Guide. You'll see some statements there that need to be completed. Let's take a moment to fill these in.

Sociologist George Herbert Mead once said, "The SELF can only exist in RELATIONSHIP to other selves."

Let's consider for a moment how God created man. Who did God want man to be in relationship with?

the compulsion for completion 11

Video:
The Compulsion for Completion

The Importance of Wholeness

Anne's Behavior

Two Lies That Sabotage Relationships

Four Components of Becoming Whole

12 SESSION ONE

Conference Call:
Two Lies That Sabotage Relationships

Sociologist George Herbert Mead once said, "The _________ can only exist in _________________ to other selves."

Lie Number One

I _______ this person to be ________________.

Lie Number Two

If this person needs _____, I will be ______________.

planning notes

Solicit brief responses from the participants. Possible answers include: *each other, God.* Use the chalkboard, overhead, or whiteboard to record responses.

We've heard Les and Leslie discuss the two lies that sabotage relationships. Let's review them.

Lie Number One

I NEED this person to be COMPLETE.

What did Les (or Leslie) have to say about this lie?

Solicit brief responses from the group.

Lie Number Two

If this person needs ME, I will be COMPLETE.

Can someone share what Les (or Leslie) had to say about this? Does this lie explain any of Anne's behavior?

Solicit brief responses from the group.

Which of these two lies is more applicable to your life—needing another person to be complete or the need to be needed? Have you ever struggled with either of these?

Solicit brief responses from the group.

5 minutes

CONFERENCE CALL: Four Steps to Becoming Whole

Please turn to page 13 in your Participant's Guide.

If you try to find INTIMACY with another person before achieving a sense of IDENTITY on your own, all your relationships become an attempt to COMPLETE YOURSELF.

In the Parrotts' book *Relationships*, they write, "The cause of our emptiness is not a case of missing persons in our lives but a case of incompletion in our soul." What do you think of that statement?

Solicit brief responses from the group.

12 SESSION ONE

Conference Call: Two Lies That Sabotage Relationships

Sociologist George Herbert Mead once said, "The _________ can only exist in _________________ to other selves."

Lie Number One

I _______ this person to be _________________.

Lie Number Two

If this person needs _____, I will be ______________.

the compulsion for completion 13

Conference Call: Four Steps to Becoming Whole

If you try to find ______________________ with another person before achieving a sense of ____________ on your own, all your relationships become an attempt to ________________________ _________________.

People who become whole learn to
heal their _________________.
remove their ______________.
sit in the __________________________.
rely on _______________.

planning notes

In the video, we heard a discussion of the four components of wholeness. Let's review them:

People who become whole learn to

heal their HURTS.
remove their MASKS.
sit in the DRIVER'S SEAT.
rely on GOD.

Now that we've had a chance to review the material presented in the video, let's take a few minutes to do some individual work.

5 minutes

ON YOUR OWN: Relational Readiness

Please turn to page 14 in your Participant's Guide.

The following individual exercise will help us evaluate how ready we are to engage in friendships and other meaningful relationships.

1. Read each statement and respond to it using the numbering system located at the top of your page.
2. Complete the exercise, then total your score.
3. Interpret your score by using the scoring paragraphs at the bottom of your page.

Any questions? You will have about 5 minutes to complete this exercise.

After 4 minutes have elapsed, warn the group they have about 1 minute left. At the end of 5 minutes, call the group back together.

5 minutes

ON YOUR OWN: Taking Off Your Masks

Please turn to page 16 in your Participant's Guide.

The following exercise is designed to assist us to become more aware of the masks we sometimes use to protect ourselves from feeling judged or negatively evaluated.

On your own, take 5 minutes to go through the three areas of work, home, and church found on pages 16–17 in your Participant's Guide. Write your responses in the appropriate places. As time permits, feel free to add other areas that pertain to your life.

On Your Own: Relational Readiness

To help you assess how ready you are to engage in friendships and other meaningful relationships, respond to each item listed below using the following scale:

4—Often
3—Sometimes
2—Seldom
1—Never

____ I feel a sense of relief when I don't have to be alone.
____ Any relationship is better than no relationship at all.
____ I experience a little bit of panic when I think of not having someone to be close to.
____ The very idea of solitude strikes fear in my heart.
____ I'm tempted to settle for any kind of friendship because I'm not sure I'll find just the right friend for me.
____ In most of my relationships, I wait to be "selected" rather than taking the initiative myself to do the selecting.
____ When I have special friendships, I feel better about myself.
____ I don't like to be alone.
____ I don't have a very clear idea of the personal qualities I look for in a person in terms of friendship.
____ If I don't have someone to be close to, I feel less complete.

Scoring: Add the numbers you have placed next to each statement. There is a possible total of forty points. To interpret your score, use the following scale:

30–40 There is a strong indication that you have a need to establish a healthier sense of your identity and personal wholeness. You will want to pay special attention to the four steps toward wholeness discussed in the video.

20–29 You have done some significant work in establishing a healthy identity and a good sense of self-worth. There's still work to do, however, in continuing to construct an integrated and whole sense of self that will help to ensure healthier relationships.

1–19 You have an established sense of security in who you are and a confident perspective on your sense of personal wholeness, which should serve you well in your relationships.

On Your Own: Taking Off Your Masks

This exercise will help you become more aware of the masks you sometimes use to guard against feeling judged or negatively evaluated. It focuses on three areas: work, home, and church. Feel free to add other areas, as well.

I wear masks at work (or school):

Very Often *Almost Never*

1 2 3 4 5 6 7

If your answer was between one and four, describe the kinds of masks you wear and with whom.

____
____
____
____

I wear masks at home:

Very Often *Almost Never*

1 2 3 4 5 6 7

If your answer was between one and four, describe the kinds of masks you wear and with whom.

____
____
____
____

I wear masks at church:

Very Often *Almost Never*

1 2 3 4 5 6 7

If your answer was between one and four, describe the kinds of masks you wear and with whom.

____
____
____
____

Any questions?

After 4 minutes, warn group members that they have 1 minute remaining. Wrap up the exercise after 5 minutes.

5 minutes

HUDDLE TIME: Masks We Wear

Please divide into small groups of three or four people, then turn to page 18 in your Participant's Guide.

Read over and discuss one or more of the three questions listed there. You will have about 5 minutes.

After 4 minutes, warn group members that they have 1 minute remaining. Wrap up the discussion after 5 minutes.

4 minutes

SESSION SUMMARY

I hope you enjoyed our first session together. We covered quite a bit of material. We investigated our relational readiness, uncovered two lies that sabotage relationships, took a look at the masks we wear in various settings and discussed ways to discard the unhealthy ones, and explored four steps we can take toward becoming whole.

Please turn to page 19 of your Participant's Guide where you will find an exercise called the "Extra Mile." Each session will have an Extra-Mile Exercise. This is an exercise to be completed at home. It's not a requirement, and we will not go over these exercises during our next session. These exercises are tools to help you apply the material to your own life—to dig a little deeper.

One of the tasks we have to do in order to become whole is to get into the driver's seat—setting a course for our lives, identifying a purpose, and following through with commitment and courage. This exercise will help you define a personal statement of purpose and then create goals to help you begin to fulfill that purpose.

I encourage all of you to complete the exercise and then discuss it with your spouse or with a friend during the week. Remember, we all seek personal significance. As the Parrotts say in their book, "This need is woven into the fabric of our nature, our very being. The desperate need for significance is as real as any physical need we ever experience."

We are, however, to rely on God, not other people, to meet our needs.

Huddle Time: Masks We Wear

- How willing and comfortable are you in disclosing yourself to others and letting yourself be known by others?
- What social masks do you sometimes wear that guard your vulnerability?
- What can you do to discard unhealthy masks? Are all masks unhealthy?

Extra-Mile Exercise

Getting into the "driver's seat"—especially when you've lived most of your life as a passenger—will take hard work, initiative, purpose, and clear-cut goals. Healthy relationships will grow out of your having an identity, a purpose, courage, and commitment.

The following exercise will help you construct a personal statement of purpose and then create goals to help you fulfill that purpose. Begin by determining what you value. Though difficult, force yourself to rank the following twelve values with "1" being the most important to you.

____ **Achievement**—feeling satisfaction from a job well done.
____ **Challenges**—using creativity, training, and intelligence to overcome obstacles.
Education—increasing your intellectual understanding of life.
____ **Aesthetics**—appreciating the beauty in people, art, or nature.
____ **Health**—feeling good in a physical and emotional sense.
____ **Independence**—having the freedom to do your own thing.
____ **Morality**—maintaining your moral, ethical, and religious standards.
____ **Pleasure**—having time to play and have a good time.
____ **Relationships**—caring for, sharing with, and giving to those close to you.
____ **Spirituality**—cultivating a meaningful and personal relationship with God.
____ **Security**—feeling safe; free from unexpected and unpleasant changes.
____ **Service to Others**—knowing you have benefited others.
____ **Wealth**—improving your financial position.

Ponder the values that are most meaningful to you. Consider how your top three or four values can be incorporated into a meaningful statement of purpose. This statement does not need to be permanent, as it will change throughout your life. For now, draft something that

seems right for you at this time in your life—something that is personally compelling and comes from the heart.

My purpose:

____
____
____

Now that your purpose statement has been drafted, note some specific and obtainable goals that will serve as a means to fulfill it.

Short-term goals (obtainable within the next three or four months)

1. ______________________________
2. ______________________________
3. ______________________________

Long-term goals (obtainable within the next year or more)

1. ______________________________
2. ______________________________
3. ______________________________

Specifically, what immediate gratifications will you have to delay in order to achieve your goals?

____
____
____
____

Example

Statement of Purpose:

To follow God's leading as I establish my career and grow in my involvement in my church.

Short-Term Goals:

1. Seek God's will through prayer, Bible reading, and journaling.
2. Meet with my supervisor to establish my career path.
3. Take a computer class to improve skills.
4. Meet with my pastor to discuss where I could minister in the church.

Long-Term Goals:

1. To be promoted within a year.
2. To be in charge of a ministry at church.

Delayed Gratification:

1. Get up earlier so as to spend daily time with God.
2. Drop chamber choir so I can take on a church ministry.
3. Save $50 a month in order to pay for computer class.

1 minute

CLOSING PRAYER

Lord, as we think about becoming whole and developing healthy relationships, help us to take the steps necessary to heal our hurts, remove our masks, sit in the driver's seat, and, most importantly, to rely on you to meet our ultimate needs. In Jesus' name, amen.

planning notes

Session Two

keeping family ties from pulling strings

BEFORE YOU LEAD

Synopsis

Our family is like a classroom where we learn the skills and knowledge that will one day enable us to live outside it. Our families teach us to trust or distrust the people around us, to speak up or stay quiet in a social setting, to give or to take. Our family sets the pattern for all other relationships.

The Compelling Power of Your Original Kin

We all started off in some sort of family. Whatever your family portrait, it's had a powerful imprint on you since day one. Literally.

Consider a baby who wakes up at three in the morning. Her mother hears her crying down the hall and comes in to tenderly comfort and nurse her. Now consider another newborn who also awoke crying in the wee hours. But this baby is met instead by a tense and tired mom. The baby starts to tense up the moment the mother pulls her from the crib.

These two scenarios are presented in a clinical report as examples of the kinds of interactions that, if repeated over and over, instill very different approaches to life and relationships. The first baby is learning that people can be trusted and counted on to help, and that she can be effective in getting help. The second baby is finding that no one really cares, that others can't be counted on, and that efforts to get help usually fail.

The point is that small exchanges between you and your family had emotional subtexts, and the messages, if left unexamined, will last a lifetime and shape every relationship you try to cultivate.

The Three Rs Every Family Teaches

It would be so convenient if the lessons our family taught were filed in an old family trunk locked away in the attic. Unfortunately, discovering just what you learned from your family is not quite that easy. Generally speaking, the lessons you learned from your family are the result of three Rs: (1) the rules they reinforced; (2) the roles they asked you to play; and (3) the relationships they modeled.

Family Rules

Each family has its own unique set of rules. And while family rules may be explicit, they are more often unspoken, operating outside the conscious awareness of every family member.

Family rules unconsciously guide individuals by describing what family members should do and how they should behave, even if they fly in the face of a person's real desires.

What unspoken rules does your family live by? Here's a sampling of the ones we hear most often:

- Don't reveal your true feelings.
- Never hide your emotions.
- Always get your point across.
- Never raise your voice.
- Do everything you can to win an argument.

Family Roles

Birth order and sibling dynamics are significant factors in shaping one's role in the family. Roles played out within the family, just like unspoken rules, often develop into lifelong patterns of behavior that influence every other relationship.

Consider the following roles to help you more accurately pinpoint your part. Which one comes closest to describing you in relationship to the rest of your family?

- Problem-solver: Always ready with a solution.
- Victim: Pulling compassion and sympathy from others.
- Rescuer: Diving into situations for somebody else's safety.
- Comedian: Ready with a joke for comic relief.
- Mediator: Serving as a bridge between others.
- Confronter: Facing reality and calling it as you see it.
- Healer: Administering healing to emotional wounds.
- Secret-keeper: Holding a confidence tight and safe.

By identifying your role in the family, you will become more empowered to fulfill it if you choose, or carve out a healthier pattern if need be.

Family Relationships

Perhaps the most powerful method our family has of teaching relationships is by example. We learn how to feel, how to think, and how to act by observing others in our home. What did you learn about relationships from the models you had at home? What did you learn about expressing affection or resolving conflict?

Where to Go from Here

Just being aware of your family's relationship lessons is not always enough to help you transcend them. A pursuit like this runs the risk of two potentially negative side effects, and it's only fair that we point them out. The first potential side effect is that you would take your new awareness only halfway. That is, that you would recognize the imprint your family legacy has left on your life and then leave it at that. We fear that you might take a helpless stance and allow your background to direct your future, thinking there is nothing you can do about it.

You're not helpless. And you are not simply a product of the way you were raised. From here on out, the kind of person you'll be is a matter of perseverance, not parenting.

The other potential side effect is worse than the first. It's that you would blame your family for the lessons they taught or didn't teach. We urge you, don't play the blame game. If you are carrying deep hurts from your family, seek the help of a competent counselor.

The bottom line is that your family—functional or dysfunctional, happy or horrific—is the launching pad for all other relationships. Take the good you can and leave the rest behind.

Session Sequence (50 minutes total)

Welcome (1 minute)
Opening Prayer (1 minute)
Review and Overview (3 minutes)
Video (8 minutes)
On Your Own (5 minutes)
Huddle Time (7 minutes)
Conference Call (5 minutes)
On Your Own (10 minutes)
Huddle Time (7 minutes)
Session Summary (2 minutes)
Closing Prayer (1 minute)

Session Two

keeping family ties from pulling strings

1 minute

WELCOME

Call the group together. Welcome the participants to Session 2 of *Relationships*: "Keeping Family Ties from Pulling Strings."

1 minute

OPENING PRAYER

Dear Father, in today's session we will be delving into our pasts—specifically our families of origin and how they have impacted our present-day relationships. For those of us for whom this may be painful, we ask for your abundant grace and love. For all of us, we ask that you open our hearts and help us consider how to use the insights we gain in order to build healthier relationships with those we care about and love. In Jesus' name, amen.

3 minutes

REVIEW AND OVERVIEW

Last week our first session was called "The Compulsion for Completion." During this session we explored our relational readiness—how ready we are to enter into a meaningful relationship with others. We also uncovered two lies that sabotage relationships—namely, "I need this person to be complete" and "If this person needs me, I will be complete." Then we took a look at the masks we wear in various settings—the ways we present ourselves in public to protect ourselves from feeling judged or negatively evaluated. And finally, we discussed ways to get rid of unhealthy masks, and we also analyzed whether all masks are unhealthy.

Please turn to page 24 in your Participant's Guide.

Session Two

keeping family ties from pulling strings

Overview

In this session you will

- review the lessons you've learned at home.
- reflect on the "unspoken rules."
- discuss how childhood lessons and rules affect our present-day relationships.

planning notes

In today's session we are going to review the lessons we've learned from our families of origin, reflect on the "unspoken rules" of our families, and discuss how childhood lessons or rules affect our present-day relationships.

8 minutes

VIDEO: Keeping Family Ties from Pulling Strings

In this video segment we'll meet Frank and Lily. They'd like to be better friends, but they're learning that they may have some differences they weren't aware of when they first met. We'll also learn about the "Three Rs" that powerfully influence our relationships, and how awareness of these can help us.

You can take notes during the video segment on page 25 of your Participant's Guide.

> Start the video; turn it off at the prompt.

Do you think Lily and Frank are mismatched? Why won't Frank be more forthcoming?

> Solicit brief responses from the group.

5 minutes

ON YOUR OWN: How Healthy Is Your Home?

Please turn to page 26 in your Participant's Guide.

According to experts, how we relate to members of our own family and how they relate to us sets the pattern for how we will relate to others. While no family is perfect, some are healthier than others. In her book *Traits of a Healthy Family*, Dolores Curran reveals the top fifteen healthy traits as noted by family experts. These are listed in your Participant's Guide on pages 26–27. To work on this exercise, use the numbering system located near the top of page 26 of your Participant's Guide. Take 5 minutes to evaluate the healthy family traits as they relate to your family of origin.

Any questions?

> After 4 minutes have elapsed, warn the group they only have 1 minute left to complete the exercise. End the exercise after 5 minutes.

Video: Keeping Family Ties from Pulling Strings

The Most Powerful Emotional System We Belong To

Frank and Lily's Relationship

The Three Rs

Family Rules

Family Roles

Family Relationships

On Your Own: How Healthy Is Your Home?

How we relate to members of our own family and how they relate to us sets the pattern for how we will relate to all other relationships. While no family is perfect, some are healthier than others. In her book *Traits of a Healthy Family*, Dolores Curran reveals the top fifteen healthy traits as repeatedly noted by family experts. They are listed below.

Using the following scale, rate the degree to which your family of origin is or was characterized by these desirable traits. (You may want to take this survey again, rating your present family situation, if applicable.)

4—Much of the time
3—Some of the time
2—Rarely
1—Almost never

Family of Origin		*Current Family*
____	Communicates and listens.	____
____	Affirms and supports one another.	____
____	Teaches respect for others.	____
____	Develops a sense of trust.	____
____	Has a sense of play and humor.	____
____	Exhibits a sense of shared responsibility.	____
____	Teaches a sense of right and wrong.	____
____	Has a strong sense of family in which rituals and traditions abound.	____
____	Has a balance of interaction among members.	____
____	Has a shared religious core.	____
____	Respects the privacy of one another.	____

____	Values service to others.	____
____	Fosters family table time and conversation.	____
____	Shares leisure time.	____
____	Admits to and seeks help with problems.	____
____	**Total**	____

Scoring: Add the numbers you have placed beside each item. There is a possible total of sixty points. To interpret your score, use the following:

50–60: Count your blessings. You grew up in a relatively loving home free of dysfunction. Your caregivers took time to nurture your development and cultivate an atmosphere that was positive and caring. Your relationships will certainly benefit from this good foundation.

30–49: Your family health falls into the midrange, or average zone. Your family of origin may not be all you would have liked it to be, but then again, things could have been a lot worse. Learn from the tensions and disengaged style that was present in your home. How did you contribute to it? What could you have done to make things better? In your present family situation, do you contribute to the tension? How? In what ways can you make things better now?

1–29: Unfortunately, this range is where you find families with the most strife. Perhaps you have experienced a lot of distressed and polarized relationships (even abusive ones) at home. If so, this will present some challenges to your present and future relationships, but nothing that can't be overcome with learning good relational skills.

7 minutes

HUDDLE TIME: Our Family of Origin

Divide into small groups of three or four people, then turn to page 28 in your Participant's Guide.

In your small groups, discuss the two questions you will find on that page. You will have about 7 minutes of discussion time.

After 6 minutes have gone by, give the group a 1-minute warning. Stop the discussion after 7 minutes have elapsed.

5 minutes

CONFERENCE CALL: The Three Rs

Finding out what we have learned from our family isn't always easy. If all the lessons could be written in a journal, we'd peruse our personal transcripts to discover the courses we'd unconsciously taken: "Feelings We Don't Talk about in This Family," "The Way We Avoid Arguments," "How We Express and Don't Express Intimacy," "Advanced Blame Shifting," and so on. The lessons we learn from our family are the result of three Rs.

Turn to page 29 in your Participant's Guide.

The three Rs every family teaches are:

RULES
ROLES
RELATIONSHIPS

On page 29 of your Participant's Guide there is a sampling of unspoken rules that many families adopt.

- Don't reveal your TRUE FEELINGS.
- Never hide your EMOTIONS.
- Always get your POINT ACROSS.
- Never raise your VOICE.
- Do everything you can to WIN AN ARGUMENT.
- COMPROMISE whenever you can.
- TRUST others only after they've earned it.
- Never call ATTENTION to yourself.
- Let others know of your ACCOMPLISHMENTS.
- Put on a HAPPY FACE.
- Always be GENUINE.

Huddle Time: Our Family of Origin

- In what ways has your family of origin shaped your personality, your career choice, your relationships, and your values?
- In what specific ways does your family still "pull your strings"? In other words, how do your early family influences still manifest themselves in your present relationships?

Conference Call: The Three Rs

Family rules unconsciously guide individuals by describing what family members should do and how they should behave, even if they fly in the face of a person's real desires.

The three Rs every family teaches are:

R________________

R________________

R________________

Samples of Unspoken Rules

- Don't reveal your ________________.
- Never hide your ________________.
- Always get your ________________.
- Never raise your ________________.
- Do everything you can to ________________.
- ________________ whenever you can.
- ________________ others only after they've earned it.
- Never call ________________ to yourself.
- Let others know your ________________.
- Put on a ________________.
- Always be ________________.

Typical Roles Played Out in a Family

- ________________: Always ready with a solution
- ________________: Pulling compassion and sympathy from others.
- ________________: Diving into situations for somebody else's safety.
- ________________: Ready with a joke for comic relief.

planning notes

Do any of those sound familiar? Now let's take a look at typical roles that are played out in a family, found on pages 29–30 of your Participant's Guide.

- PROBLEM-SOLVER—Always ready with a solution.
- VICTIM—Pulling compassion and sympathy from others.
- RESCUER—Diving into situations for somebody else's safety.
- COMEDIAN—Ready with a joke for comic relief.
- MEDIATOR—Serving as a bridge between others.
- CONFRONTER—Facing reality and calling it as you see it.
- HEALER—Administering healing to emotional wounds.
- SECRET-KEEPER—Holding a confidence tight and safe.

10 minutes

ON YOUR OWN: Lessons Learned from Mom and Dad

Please turn to page 31 in your Participant's Guide. This 10-minute exercise is designed to help you evaluate how each of your parents—or primary caregivers—behaved.

Rate their effectiveness in each of the categories on a scale of 1 to 10, with 1 being the least effective.

As time allows, write a brief description of how each person performed each skill. We will use this exercise as a basis for our small-group discussion, which will follow.

After about 9 minutes have elapsed, give your class a 1-minute warning. After 10 minutes, conclude the exercise.

7 minutes

HUDDLE TIME: How Our Families Have Influenced Our Relationships

Divide into small groups of three or four, then turn to page 32 in your Participant's Guide.

In your small groups, discuss the two questions you will find on that page. You will have about 7 minutes.

After about 6 minutes have elapsed, give your class a 1-minute warning. After 7 minutes, conclude the exercise.

- ____________________: Serving as a bridge between others.
- ____________________: Facing reality and calling it as you see it.
- ____________________: Administering healing to emotional wounds.
- ____________________: Holding a confidence tight and safe.

On Your Own:
Lessons Learned from Mom and Dad

The following exercise will help you evaluate how each of your parents (or primary caregivers) behaved. Take about ten minutes to rate their effectiveness on a scale of one to ten, with one being the least effective. As time allows, write a brief description of how each person performed each skill.

Category	*Mother*	*Father*
Talking about his/her experiences	____	____
Showing his/her feelings	____	____
Standing up for himself/herself	____	____
Being a good listener	____	____
Understanding others' perspectives	____	____
Managing anger	____	____
Accepting responsibility (not passing the buck)	____	____
Working for equitable solutions	____	____

Huddle Time:
How Our Families Have Influenced Our Relationships

- In what ways has your family of origin influenced the relationships you have with other people today?
- Of the three major ways families shape us—rules, roles, and relationships—which one do you see as the most influential for you and why?

2 minutes

SUMMARY

We have covered a lot of material in this session. We reviewed the lessons we have learned from our families of origin, reflected on the "unspoken rules," and discussed how childhood lessons or rules affect our present-day relationships.

Please turn to page 33 in your Participant's Guide.

For those of you who want to do some extra work on your own, this special Extra-Mile Exercise will help you investigate the unspoken rules in your family of origin. After you have completed the exercise, discuss it with your spouse or a special friend.

As was true last week, we will not be going over the Extra-Mile Exercise in class. It is intended to help you apply what we've learned in class—to help you dig deeper.

1 minute

CLOSING PRAYER

Lord, grant us wisdom as we reflect on what we've discussed today. Help us to apply what we've learned toward building healthier relationships with those we love. Help us to evaluate the lessons we've learned from our families of origin with openness and honesty. Help us see things through your eyes, and guide us toward being more like you. In Jesus' name, amen.

Extra-Mile Exercise

What were the unspoken rules in your family of origin? The following exercise will help you pinpoint some of the rules you may have absorbed. Complete the following sentence stems with whatever first pops into your mind.

Men should ______________________________

Women should ______________________________

Success is ______________________________

The most important thing is ______________________________

Life ______________________________

Now review what you have written and edit it to conform to how you believe your parents would have completed these sentences. This will give you a pretty good start at uncovering your family's unspoken rules. Use the space below to write any additional rules that may not have been articulated but were still known.

In what specific ways do your family's unspoken rules influence your relationships?

planning notes

Session Three

crossing the gender line

BEFORE YOU LEAD

Synopsis

The barrier between the sexes is built early in life by our fear of being teased for having a "girlfriend" or "boyfriend." Remember those days? Some researchers can't seem to forget. A classic study of children's friendships has found that three-year-olds say about half their friends are of the opposite sex; for five-year-olds it's about twenty percent, and by age seven almost no boys or girls say they have a best friend of the opposite sex.

This chapter is dedicated to helping you take some of the mystery out of relating to the opposite sex. We start with a straightforward fact: When men and women get together there are, in effect, two worlds—his and hers. The question this raises, however, is: What's the difference?

A World of Difference

Have you ever wondered why a man can seemingly read a map blindfolded but can't find his own socks? The reason may be found in his genetic makeup. Research is discovering that men and women actually perceive reality differently.

Why are researchers just now exploring the differences between men and women? The reason can be traced to the 1970s when the feminist revolution nearly prohibited talk of inborn differences in the behavior of males and females. But as hard as we tried to squelch our differences, the evidence for innate gender difference began to mount, and admitting the differences between men and women has now become unavoidable. What's more, the differences are not exclusively relegated to how you were raised as a child and society's traditional stereotyping. The differences, research is discovering, may lie much deeper.

It turns out that men's and women's brains, for example, are not only different, but the way we use our brains differs too. Women have larger connections and subsequently more frequent "cross talk" between their brain's left and right hemispheres. This accounts for women's seeming ability to have better verbal skills and relational intuition than men. Men, on the other hand, have greater brain hemisphere separation, which enhances abstract reasoning and visual-spatial intelligence.

What Women Need to Know about Men

If you are a woman reading this, I (Leslie) want to reveal a few facts that can help you make healthy connections with the men in your life. Of course, there are always exceptions to the rule, but generally speaking, here are a few of the important distinctions.

- *Men are not as in touch with their emotions as we are*. I'm not saying they don't feel things deeply, but men certainly don't express their emotions as clearly or as readily as we do.
- *Men are more independent than we are*. Very early on, males define themselves in relation to their mothers by being different and separate. Their impulse is to go away and assert their masculinity.
- *Men are more abstract than we are*. While you and I are more likely to talk about our fears, feelings, and experiences, men are more likely to talk about ideas, concepts, and theories. Men want to tell you what they know.

What Men Need to Know about Women

Now that Leslie has had her say, allow me (Les) to turn the tables. Just as there are important insights for women to gain in understanding men, so can you, as a male reader, discover a few tips that will make relating to the women in your life a bit easier.

- *Women are not as independent as we are*. Let's face it: we love the mystique of the rugged "Marlboro Man" image. Sure it's cliché, but we can't get over this tough-minded, lone cowboy who reports to nobody as he freely rides the range. Women, on the other hand, could care less about protecting their autonomy.
- *Women focus on the here-and-now more than we do*. While we are scheming plans and solving problems for a better tomorrow, most women are asking, "What's going on right now, and how do I (and others) feel about it?" Women focus on current feelings and experiences because these build emotional bonds of connection between them.
- *Women are not as competitive as we are*. As men, we want to prove our point, keep score, and win the debate in conversation, while women are more likely to sacrifice superiority as the price for keeping peace.

Can Men and Women Be Just Friends?

For many people, the idea of a man and a woman being friends is charming, but improbable. "It always leads to something else," they argue, meaning that the relationship eventually becomes romantic or soon fizzles out. Perhaps they are right.

On the other hand, there are those who are seemingly surprised by the question and argue that of course male-female friendships are possible. These people's persuasiveness almost makes the romantic pull of such relationships seem unusual.

In our informal survey of people who are "just friends" with someone of the opposite sex, we heard a number of positive remarks. Over and over, men spoke about how a woman's friendship provided them with a kind of nurturance not generally available in their relationships with men.

Interestingly, women do not report the same level of intimacy as men do with their cross-gender friendships. Even women who count men among their close friends feel barriers between them.

So does all this mean the answer to the question about men and women being friends is yes? Few relationship issues are that plain and simple. The real answer is, "it depends"—upon how much each person in the relationship is willing to stretch and grow.

Session Sequence (50 minutes total)

Welcome (2 minutes)
Opening Prayer (1 minute)
Review and Overview (2 minutes)
Video (7 minutes)
Conference Call (5 minutes)
On Your Own (5 minutes)
On Your Own (10 minutes)
Huddle Time (10 minutes)
Conference Call (5 minutes)
Session Summary (2 minutes)
Closing Prayer (1 minute)

Session Three

crossing the gender line

2 minutes

WELCOME

Call the group together. Welcome the participants to Session 3 of *Relationships*: "Crossing the Gender Line."

1 minute

OPENING PRAYER

Thank you, Lord, for creating us—male and female—in your image. As we examine the information in today's session, help us gain new insights and perspective. May the truths we discover bring us closer to understanding how uniquely you have made us, and help us to appreciate our differences as men and women. In Jesus' name, amen.

2 minutes

REVIEW AND OVERVIEW

During Session 2, "Keeping Family Ties from Pulling Strings," we talked about the lessons we learned from our families of origin. We learned about the three Rs: the *rules* they reinforced, the *roles* they asked us to play, and the *relationships* they modeled.

We also discussed how childhood lessons and rules affect our present-day relationships. The authors said, "The bottom line is that your family—functional or dysfunctional—is the launching pad for all other relationships."

Please turn to page 36 of your Participant's Guide for an overview of today's session.

Today we will discover our gender differences, examine what men need to know about women and what women need to know about men, and discuss what it would be like to be the opposite sex.

Session Three

crossing the gender line

Overview

In this session you will

- discover gender differences.
- examine what women need to know about men.
- explore what men need to know about women.
- discuss what it would be like to be the opposite sex.

planning notes

7 minutes

VIDEO: Crossing the Gender Line

In this video segment Leslie begins with one of her favorite stories that illustrates the differences in the way men and women see the world. Then we revisit Anne and Tom, whom we met in the first session. As you will see, they're trying to work out some of their differences.

Please turn to page 37 in your Participant's Guide to take notes on the video.

Start the video; turn it off at the prompt.

Do you think part of Tom and Anne's communication problem is gender based? Is either of them wrong?

5 minutes

CONFERENCE CALL: Exploring Our Gender Roles

We're going to spend 5 minutes discussing the two questions found on page 38 of your Participant's Guide. Let's start with the men, and then we'll wrap it up with the women responding.

1. Think about your cross-gender relationships, either past or present. What aspects of those relationships with the opposite sex (excluding romantic relationships) seem to be easier than relationships with the same sex?
2. When you were growing up, what social activities or games influenced your perception of gender roles?

5 minutes

ON YOUR OWN: What's Your Gender IQ?

Please turn to page 39 in your Participant's Guide.

This exercise will test our awareness of some fundamental differences between men and women. Take 5 minutes to respond to the ten statements listed on the page. Circle T for true or F for false. Then score your answers using the scoring key at the bottom of the page.

After 4 minutes have elapsed, warn the group that they only have 1 minute left to complete the exercise. Conclude the exercise after 5 minutes.

Let's have a show of hands. How many answered all ten correctly? How many got nine? Eight? One?

Video: Crossing the Gender Line

Leslie's Story about Winnie the Pooh and Piglet

Anne and Tom in the Gym

Men Tend to Be

Women Tend to Be

Importance of Simple Communication and Sharing

Conference Call: Exploring Our Gender Roles

- Consider your cross-gender relationships. What aspects of these relationships with the opposite sex (excluding romantic relationships) seem to be easier than relationships with the same sex?
- When you were growing up, what social activities or games influenced your perception of gender roles?

On Your Own: What's Your Gender IQ?

How much do you know about the fundamental differences between men and women? Label the following statements as either true or false to find out how much you already know.

T F Women are better spellers than men.
T F Men are more likely than women to use conversation to solve problems.
T F Women have larger connections between their brain's left and right hemispheres.
T F Men are better at reading the emotions of others than women are.
T F Men score higher on the math section of the SAT than do women.
T F In comparison to men, women are better at maintaining a sense of geographical location.
T F Men are better than women at fitting suitcases into a crowded car trunk.
T F Women are better than men at describing their feelings.
T F Men, more than women, focus their energy on achievement.
T F Women, more than men, give priority to relationships.

Scoring: Each of these statements are based on current gender research studies. The correct answers are: 1-T, 2-T, 3-T, 4-F, 5-T, 6-F, 7-T, 8-T, 9-T, 10-T. The more items you answered correctly, the better your knowledge of gender differences.

10 minutes

ON YOUR OWN: What If You Were the Opposite Sex?

Please turn to page 40 in your Participant's Guide.

Learning about the opposite sex and seeing things from their perspective are two different things. This 10-minute exercise will help us to at least begin to see things from the viewpoint of the opposite gender. Women, answer the questions as if you were a man. Men, answer the question as if you were a woman.

After 9 minutes have gone by, give a 1-minute warning. Conclude the exercise after 10 minutes have elapsed.

10 minutes

HUDDLE TIME: What It Would Be Like to Be the Opposite Sex

Break into small groups of three or four people.

Was it easy for you to imagine being a member of the opposite gender? What made it easy or difficult for you? Take the next 10 minutes to discuss your responses.

At the 9-minute mark, warn the group they have only 1 minute left to conclude their discussion. End the small-group session after 10 minutes.

5 minutes

CONFERENCE CALL: What It Would Be Like to Be the Opposite Sex

Come back together as a large group; ask a spokesperson from each group to briefly report responses and insights from the Huddle Time. End discussion after 5 minutes.

On Your Own: What If You Were the Opposite Sex?

Take fifteen minutes to put yourself into the shoes of the opposite sex. If you are a man, imagine what it would be like for you to be a woman. If you are a woman, how would being a man change your perspective? Be as honest as you can as you answer the following questions.

1. What is your first reaction to living as the opposite sex?

2. How would the simple task of getting ready in the morning be different if you were the opposite gender? Take into consideration the time it would take, what you would do, how you would dress.

3. How would living as the opposite sex affect your career choice and other aspirations?

4. As the opposite gender, would you feel more or less safe in society? Why?

5. Would you feel any different about marriage or relationships with the opposite sex if you were the opposite gender? If so, how?

6. How would your relationship with both your parents differ if you were the opposite gender?

Share your responses in your small-group discussion.

planning notes

2 minutes

SESSION SUMMARY

During today's session we discovered our gender differences, examined what men need to know about women and what women need to know about men, and discussed what it would be like to be the opposite sex.

Please turn to page 42 in your Participant's Guide.

As with Sessions 1 and 2, this one comes with an Extra-Mile Exercise for you to complete on your own at home, during the week. This exercise will provide you with the opportunity to do some more self-examination. It is highly recommended that you share your responses with your spouse or a close friend.

1 minute

CLOSING PRAYER

Thank you, Lord, for giving men and women such unique qualities and characteristics. Help us to appreciate each other, to learn more from each other, and to develop a sense of tolerance and patience in our relationships. Above all, help us to see your characteristics in each other because we know we are each created—male and female—in your image. In Jesus' name we pray, amen.

42 SESSION THREE

Extra-Mile Exercise

Do some more self-examination. If possible, share your responses with your spouse or a close friend.

1. Describe your experience of completing the exercises for this session. What did you learn about yourself?

2. This session noted several things men and women should know about each other. What differences can you add?

3. Women use their conversation to build "rapport," while men use conversation to give or get a "report." Cite examples from your own experience that support this statement.

4. We doom relationships with the opposite sex when we try to change them into becoming more like us. What can you do to accept and even appreciate the different qualities of the other gender?

planning notes

Session Four

friends to die for

BEFORE YOU LEAD

Synopsis

I would never have imagined that a thirty-year friendship could begin in a church nursery between two toddlers. But it did. I had found a kindred spirit. Laura was indeed to become the best friend of my childhood, my bunk partner at summer camp, my college roommate, and my maid-of-honor at my wedding. Laura is truly a friend to die for.

I couldn't have known at age five, of course, how precious this kind of friendship is and how rarely I would find it in my life. But most people do, in fact, find a kindred spirit or two.

This chapter stands as a tribute to friendship and is dedicated to helping you raise your current relationships to their highest pitch of enjoyment and to building a firm foundation for prospective friends in your future.

What Friends Are For

In the biblical creation story, the Creator, having formed the first person, immediately declared our social character: "It is not good that man should be alone."

Seventeenth-century philosopher Francis Bacon noted two tremendously positive effects of friendship: "It redoubleth joys, and cutteth griefs in half."

There's exciting news about having a kindred spirit these days. Not only are friends good for the soul but for the body as well. Friends help us ward off depression, boost our immune system, lower our cholesterol, increase the odds of surviving with coronary disease, and keep stress hormones in check. What's more, research is showing that you can extend your life expectancy by having the right kind of friends.

The few good friends we enjoy generally come in one of two forms, both desirable and equally delightful. They are friends of the road and friends of the heart.

Friends of the Road

How does a once-bosom buddy wind up a distant memory? And is a friendship that fades away necessarily a bad thing? I don't think so.

Some friendships are meant to be transitory. Like cowboys who ride the herd together for miles, sharing both dusty perils and round-the-campfire coffee, we all have friendships that come to their natural end. Not because of discontent or lack of interest, but simply because the road has run out. We've hit the end of the trail together, and it's time to move on to other things, other companies of men.

Understand, these are not failed friendships. Not at all. They are friendships of the road, equally intense, equally necessary, equally worth cultivating and treasuring as the long-lasting versions.

Friends of the Heart

There's nothing like a friend of the heart, long-lasting pals who know us sometimes better than we know ourselves. They bring such comfort to our lives, it's nearly inexpressible.

Of course, we don't usually determine that a specific relationship will outlast the road. Some do, some don't. In ancient times, friends vowed to be friends forever, no matter what. Maybe you remember the biblical story of Jonathan and David and how they took an oath to be friends forever.

Are friendships of the heart more important than our fleeting friends of the road? Not really. We need both. What matters is how a relationship sustains you right now. An achieved friendship—of any brand or bond—is among the best experiences life has to offer.

How We Find True Friends

Friendship is a long conversation. Indeed, the ability to generate good talk by the hour is the most promising indication, during the uncertain early stages, that a possible friendship will take hold.

The pressure to achieve "quality" communication, however, sometimes induces a sort of inauthentic epiphany for overeager friends-to-be (not unlike what sometimes happens with an eager-to-please patient in the last ten minutes of a psychotherapy session). If authenticity does not enter in soon, the two parties form an uneasy kind of pseudofriendship that creates more pretense than pleasure. With the proper techniques, people can break free of pseudo-friendship and achieve true companionship.

The first important technique is to master the art of good talk. This requires just two simple tools: a listening ear and self-disclosure.

Some people are especially skilled at opening others up. They readily elicit intimacy because they listen well. But knowing when and how to talk about yourself is as important a skill as listening. No one really gets close to the kind of person who's so careful about her image she never reveals anything intimate.

How We Keep True Friends

It's one thing to start a friendship, it's quite another to maintain it. It's so easy to take good friends for granted. And in a sense, we should. Like a comfortable pair of gloves, old friends wear well. But friendships that suffer from busyness and overfamiliarity can't afford to be neglected too long. They need renewal. Research has revealed the qualities that keep true friendship alive and well.

- *Loyalty*. The quality that tops the list in survey after survey of what people appreciate most about their friends is loyalty.
- *Forgiveness*. Every friend you'll ever have will eventually disappoint you. Count on it. That doesn't mean that every offense of a friend requires forgiveness; some slights need only be overlooked and forgotten.
- *Honesty*. Honesty is not only expressed in words; it means being authentic. True friends aren't afraid to be honest and they aren't afraid to be themselves.
- *Dedication*. The meaning of dedication refers to the ability of two people to influence each other's plans, thoughts, actions, and emotions. Personal sacrifice. Selfless devotion. Commitment. These are the noble qualities dedication requires.

Session Sequence (50 minutes total)

Welcome (2 minutes)

Opening Prayer (1 minute)

Review and Overview (1 minute)

Video (8 minutes)

On Your Own (10 minutes)

On Your Own (5 minutes)

Huddle Time (13 minutes)

Conference Call (7 minutes)

Session Summary (2 minutes)

Closing Prayer (1 minute)

Session Four

friends to die for

2 minutes

WELCOME

Call the group together. Welcome the participants to Session 4 of *Relationships*: "Friends to Die For."

1 minute

OPENING PRAYER

Dear Father, in your wisdom you have created us to be social beings. We need to be in relationship—first to you and then to one another. Thank you for the relationships you have given us here on earth. Help us to cultivate good and healthy friendships. In Jesus' name, amen.

1 minute

REVIEW AND OVERVIEW

During our last session, we discovered some gender differences. God created men and women to be different—not only physically but also in the way we react, our needs, our ways of communicating, and how we view relationships. We also examined what women need to know about men and what men need to know about women. Then we discussed what it would be like to go through the day as a member of the opposite sex. I hope that many of you completed the Extra-Mile Exercise during the week and had a chance to talk about your responses to your spouse or to a friend.

Please turn to page 44 in your Participant's Guide for our session overview.

During Session 4, we are going to investigate what friends are for, determine what are the right kinds of friends, discover how good friends are made, and discuss the qualities that comprise a good friendship.

Session Four

friends to die for

Overview

In this session you will

- explore how much you can expect from a friend.
- examine why and how friends fail.
- look at five steps to take toward reconciliation.

planning notes

8 minutes

VIDEO: Friends to Die For

Today's video segment introduces two types of friendships: friends of the road and friends of the heart. We'll look more closely at a special friendship—Lily and Bette demonstrate the ups and downs of great friendships. And Les and Leslie Parrott will define some of the qualities that make some people the "friends to die for."

There is space provided for taking notes on page 45 in your Participant's Guide.

> Start the video; turn it off at the prompt.

Let's review the video for a moment with a couple of questions.

Can those who love us the most also hurt us the most?

Is honesty always the best policy?

> Solicit brief responses from the group.

10 minutes

ON YOUR OWN: The Friendship Assessment

Please turn to page 46 in your Participant's Guide.

The following exercise will help us evaluate the current condition of three friendships we have. If you wish to evaluate more than three friendships, you may do so during the coming week. Read each of the statements on pages 46–47 of your Participant's Guide and determine whether it is true or false for each friend you evaluate. You will have 10 minutes to work on this exercise.

> After 9 minutes have gone by, warn the group that they have 1 minute remaining. Conclude the exercise after 10 minutes have elapsed.

Video: Friends to Die For

Friendship Actually Cures Stress

Friends of the Road

Friends of the Heart

Lily and Bette Working It Out

Qualities That Make a Great Friend

On Your Own: The Friendship Assessment

This exercise will help you evaluate the current condition of each of your friendships. Take ten minutes to evaluate one to three friendships. You can always go back and evaluate other friendships on your own. Read each statement and determine if it is true or false for each friend you are evaluating.

Answer T or F

Friend #1	*Friend #2*	*Friend #3*	*Characteristics*
___	___	___	This person knows how to keep a secret.
___	___	___	We can disagree and then make up without holding grudges.
___	___	___	This person almost always makes time for me, and I do the same for him/her.
___	___	___	When he/she gives me advice, it is generally without judgment.
___	___	___	I can totally be myself around this person.
___	___	___	He/she is a good listener.
___	___	___	This person has stuck by me through tough times and is willing to make personal sacrifices for me.
___	___	___	This person knows my faults but loves me anyway.
___	___	___	Our relationship is balanced with give and take; we are equally vulnerable and caring.
___	___	___	I am able to set clear boundaries with this person when necessary, and he/she respects them.
___	___	___	No subject is off-limits in our conversation.

___	___	___	I can always count on this person.
___	___	___	**Total Number of T Responses**

Scoring: Add up the number of true responses for each friendship you evaluated. There is a possible total of twelve points for each relationship. Interpret your score using the following:

10–12 No doubt about it, this is a good friend who is worth all the effort, care, and investigation. You will want to do all that you can to nurture this relationship and enjoy it.

7–9 Though this person could be more sensitive to your needs, this friend shows great potential. Be careful, however, not to set yourself up for disappointment if this person doesn't meet all your expectations.

0–6 This friend is probably too fair-weather to see you through stormy times (and maybe even the sunny ones too). Don't hang all your hopes on this one.

5 minutes

ON YOUR OWN: Are You a "Growth-Promoting" Listener?

Please turn to page 48 in your Participant's Guide, where we will complete the statements shown.

Friendship is a long CONVERSATION. Indeed, the ability to generate good talk by the hour is the most promising indication, during the uncertain early stages, that a possible friendship will take hold.

There are two skills needed in carrying on a good conversation. The first one is the ability to LISTEN. The second one is SELF-DISCLOSURE.

For now, we are going to focus on the first skill—listening.

This second exercise will help us determine how strong our listening skills are. Take 5 minutes to answer the three items listed on pages 48–49 as honestly as you can. Add up the numbers you've circled and use the scoring section to interpret your score.

After 4 minutes have elapsed, give the class a 1-minute warning. Conclude the exercise after 5 minutes have gone by.

13 minutes

HUDDLE TIME: Assessing Friendships

Please break into small groups of three to four people each.

Now, turn to page 50 in your Participant's Guide. Take 13 minutes to discuss the questions about our friendships.

Give the class 12 minutes to talk and then issue a 1-minute warning. After 13 minutes, conclude the small-group discussion.

On Your Own: Are You a "Growth-Promoting" Listener?

Friendship is a long ____________________.

Indeed, the ability to generate good talk by the hour is the most promising indication, during the uncertain early stages, that a possible friendship will take hold.

There are two skills needed in carrying on a good conversation. The first one is the ability to ________________. The second one is ________________.

This second exercise assesses your strengths and areas for growth when it comes to the important friendship skill of listening. It is important that you be honest in answering each of the following three items.

1. Generally speaking, in meeting someone for the first time, are you *genuinely* interested in getting to know that person and understanding his/her story? Do you really want to know what interests that person? Or are you more likely to just go through the motions, being socially appropriate but not very genuine?

   Not Genuine *Extremely Genuine*

   1 2 3 4 5 6 7

2. Generally speaking, in meeting someone for the first time, are you *accepting* of that person's opinions and feelings? Do you feel open to hearing what he or she has to say, or are you more likely to interject your opinions and feelings before completely understanding the other person's?

   Not Genuine *Extremely Genuine*

   1 2 3 4 5 6 7

3. Generally speaking, in meeting someone for the first time, are you *empathic* with him or her? Do you put yourself in the other person's shoes and try to accurately understand his or her experience, or are you more likely to jump to a few conclusions and make a few assumptions?

   Not Genuine *Extremely Genuine*

   1 2 3 4 5 6 7

____Total Score

Scoring: Add up the numbers you have circled. There is a total of twenty-one points possible. The higher your score, the more likely you are to be a growth-promoting listener. However, you may find it more helpful to consider each continuum separately to see which of the three important qualities you will want to work on most.

Huddle Time: Assessing Friendships

- It has been said that many people audition to be our friends but only a few make the cut. What is it about your friends that helped them "get the part"?
- Did it have more to do with circumstances or personal attributes?
- What were the circumstances or personal attributes?

7 minutes

CONFERENCE CALL: The Top Quality in a Friendship

It's one thing to start a friendship, it's quite another to maintain it. It's so easy to take good friends for granted. And in a sense, we should. Like a comfortable pair of gloves, old friends wear well. But friendships that suffer from busyness and overfamiliarity can't afford to be neglected too long. They need renewal. Research has revealed the qualities that keep true friendship alive and well.

Let's take a look at four qualities that are essential to any friendship, filling in the statements shown on page 51 in your Participant's Guide:

- The quality that tops the list in survey after survey of what people appreciate most about their friends is LOYALTY.
- Every friend you'll ever have will eventually disappoint you. Count on it. That doesn't mean that every offense of a friend requires FORGIVENESS; some slights need only be overlooked and forgotten.
- HONESTY is not only expressed in words; it means being authentic. True friends aren't afraid to be honest and they aren't afraid to be themselves.
- The meaning of DEDICATION refers to the ability of two people to influence each other's plans, thoughts, actions, and emotions. Personal sacrifice. Selfless devotion. Commitment. These are the noble qualities dedication requires.

Of the four qualities Les and Leslie mentioned, which quality is the most important to you and why?

Solicit brief responses from the group.

2 minutes

SESSION SUMMARY

During Session 4 we investigated what friends are for, determined what are the right kinds of friends, discovered how good friends are made, and discussed the qualities that comprise a good friendship.

Please turn to page 52 in your Participant's Guide.

This week, I'd like you to seriously consider completing the Extra-Mile Exercise. It will help you determine what kind of friend you are. When reading the statements, respond the way you think your friends would respond about you.

Conference Call: The Top Quality in a Friendship

Let's take a look at four qualities that are essential to any friendship:

- The quality that tops the list in survey after survey of what people appreciate most about their friends is ____________.
- Every friend you'll ever have will eventually disappoint you. Count on it. That doesn't mean that every offense of a friend requires ________________________; some slights need only be overlooked and forgotten.
- ____________________ is not only expressed in words; it means being authentic. True friends aren't afraid to be honest, and they aren't afraid to be themselves.
- The meaning of ________________________ refers to the ability of two people to influence each other's plans, thoughts, actions, and emotions. Personal sacrifice. Selfless devotion. Commitment. These are the noble qualities dedication requires.
- Of the four qualities mentioned in the video, which is the most important one for you, and why?

Extra-Mile Exercise

This exercise will help you evaluate what kind of a friend *you* are. Consider what your friends would say about you when it comes to the following statements. Answer yes or no to each of these items as honestly as you can.

My friends would say . . .

Y N I always keep my promises.
Y N I always stick up for them.
Y N I give them grace when they let me down.
Y N I am just as likely to genuinely celebrate my friends' successes as I am to comfort them in their disappointments.
Y N I am there when they need me.
Y N I never gossip about them or talk behind their back.
Y N I give them the benefit of the doubt.
Y N I hear them out even when I disagree.
Y N I stand by them through thick and thin.

Scoring: The more items you honestly responded to with a yes, the more likely you are to be loyal to your friends. If you answered yes to nearly all of the items, however, you probably shouldn't take this quality in yourself for granted. Check in with your friends. Ask them to give you a loyalty checkup by inviting them to give honest feedback on how you are doing with being loyal.

On the other hand, if you did not answer yes to very many of these items, you may want to talk to your friends about how you can better cultivate this quality. Remember, loyalty is what tops the list of what people appreciate most about their friends, so this is one you will want to spend some time on.

planning notes

1 minute

CLOSING PRAYER

Lord, help us to exhibit the four qualities good friends should have: loyalty, the ability to forgive, honesty, and dedication. In our conversations, help us to be good listeners—caring listeners—especially to those who mean the most to us. In Jesus' name, amen.

planning notes

Session Five

what to do when friends fail

BEFORE YOU LEAD

Synopsis

Most friendships that fade are gone forever. Very few are strong enough to make us wish for a second chance.

There are times when all of us look closely at a friendship and realize that it just isn't working. It may be a fairly new friendship that still has a few wrinkles in it, or it may be a longtime friendship that was once rock solid but now appears to be fracturing.

This chapter is an attempt to learn not only why but how friends sometimes fail. We'll take a hard look at irreconcilable differences (both real and imagined) and give you practical tools for determining whether a sinking friendship has any chance of staying afloat.

How Much Can You Expect from a Friend?

Why start with a question? Because your answer is a pretty good barometer of how well your friendships will weather relational storms. Let's face it, we don't ask much of casual friendships, the kind in which you invite each other to a party once a year. But we demand more than you might guess from friendships characterized by strong feelings and a shared history. We expect friendships to be easier, more automatic than they actually are.

Think about your childhood friendships. They often set the tone for all the rest. You never "worked" on first-grade friendships, they just happened.

Why Friends Fail

Why would a once sturdy and fulfilling friendship suddenly, or even gradually, falter? The answer is actually rather straightforward. Most friendships break for one of three main reasons: a major change such as marriage or a move; neglect; or the betrayal of a confidence.

- *Change*. The change factor is part emotional and part practical. Since most friendships begin when both people are going through similar experiences, when something big happens to change the status of one friend, it's human nature for the other to feel some envy—"Why her and not me?"

- *Neglect.* Some friendships die because they aren't moving forward. They die from stagnation or plain old neglect. You meant to call but didn't. But friendships need to be nurtured. Without nurturance, annoyance is sure to set in.
- *Betrayal.* When a once-trusted confidant double-crosses you, betrayal is the result. And while change and neglect may be more common reasons for failed friendships, betrayal is almost always more painful. Why? Because betrayal dismantles trust.

Mending Broken Friendships

If you have a long-lost friend with whom things ended badly, you may be able to make a meaningful reconnection. The following five-step plan will help you determine whether or not a particular friendship should be saved and, if so, how you can do it.

- *Step One: Count the cost.* You must determine whether your fractured friendship should be repaired. An unhealthy relationship is not worth repairing if it forces you to compromise your principles or subvert your self-respect. If you sense that a friendship is unhealthy for you but keep pursuing it, we urge you to assess your relational neediness. If, on the other hand, your friendship is worth the cost of repairing and maintaining—if it has redeeming qualities you value—you're ready for the next step.
- *Step Two: Make meaningful contact.* If you've decided it's wise to reestablish contact, you need to write a note or call the person to convey one primary message: "Our friendship is valuable to me, and I miss seeing you. Is there any way we can resolve what stands between us?" It is impossible to be humble and make meaningful contact in a genuine way if you are hanging on to anger and resentment. There is a key to releasing these toxic emotions, however, and it is found in the next step.
- *Step three: Forgive as best you can.* When someone slights you, offends you, or deeply hurts you, the urge to respond in kind is natural. The problem with this urge is that we don't know when to stop. Forgiveness puts an end to all that. It begins by setting our pride aside and trying our best to see the situation from the other person's perspective. And remember, the truth is we can never balance the scales. "Do not repay anyone evil for evil," says the apostle Paul, instead "live at peace." That's the result of forgiveness: peace. Sweet peace. And it sets the tone for the next step in repairing your friendship.
- *Step Four: Diagnose the problem.* One of the reasons we avoid diagnosing the problem is that we don't like to acknowledge that there is a problem. We know that "everybody's human," but we often assign larger-than-life qualities to certain individuals, and if they are a "good friend" we see them as all good, but when they let us down we tend to see them as all bad. Don't pretend there's no problem. Diagnose it together and move to the next step.
- *Step Five: Rebuild respect.* Roman statesman and philosopher Cicero, who wrote perhaps the best treatise ever on friendship, insisted that what brings

true friends together is "a mutual belief in each other's goodness." This insistence on virtue as a precondition for true friendship may seem difficult to cultivate when a friend has let you down, but it is essential. That's why the final step in mending a broken relationship is rebuilding respect for your friend. Begin by noting your friend's most admirable qualities. Make a list of these qualities of character. Next, you need to own up to your end of the relationship by offering a sincere apology for not being the kind of friend you could have been. Identify specific things you did that contributed to the friendship's failure and confess them to your friend in an apology.

Session Sequence (50 minutes total)

Welcome (1 minute)
Opening Prayer (1 minute)
Review and Overview (2 minutes)
Video (9 minutes)
On Your Own (5 minutes)
Conference Call (5 minutes)
On Your Own (9 minutes)
Huddle Time (5 minutes)
Conference Call (10 minutes)
Session Summary (2 minutes)
Closing Prayer (1 minute)

Session Five

what to do when friends fail

1 minute

WELCOME

Call the group together. Welcome the participants to Session 5 of *Relationships*: "What to Do When Friends Fail."

1 minute

OPENING PRAYER

Dear Father, even though you never fail us, you know that sometimes our friends do fail us or we fail them. Your own Son, Jesus Christ, understood what it meant to have friends who turned away. Help us to learn and grow from failed friendships, and to restore those friendships we can. In Jesus' name, amen.

2 minutes

REVIEW AND OVERVIEW

Session 4 helped us look at friendships—how they're formed and what qualities go into good friendships. We investigated what friends are for—their importance and the fact that we were created to enjoy relationships with other people. We looked at the right kinds of friends. We also discovered that there are basically two kinds of friends: those of the road and those of the heart. Then we took a look at how good friends are made—which starts with conversation. We learned about two simple techniques for mastering the art of good talk: a listening ear and self-disclosure. Finally we took a look at the qualities that comprise a good friendship: loyalty, forgiveness, honesty, and dedication.

Please turn to page 54 in your Participant's Guide for our session overview.

This week we're going to take a look at friendships that fail. During this session we will explore how much we can expect from a friend and examine why and how friends fail. Then we're going to look at five steps we can take to reconcile a failed or damaged relationship.

Session Five

what to do when friends fail

Overview

In this session you will

- explore how much you can expect from a friend.
- examine why and how friends fail.
- look at five steps to take toward reconciliation.

planning notes

9 minutes

VIDEO: What to Do When Friends Fail

In the previous session, we saw that even a great friendship has ups and downs. In this session, we'll see a worse case—when a friendship looks like it's failing. It seems Frank, who's been seeing a lot of Lily lately, is not spending much time with his friend Mark. Do they let their friendship fail or try to resurrect it?

We'll look at three reasons why friends fail, and steps you can take to save them.

There is space provided for taking notes on page 55 in your Participant's Guide.

Start the video; turn it off at the prompt.

Should Mark talk about this problem? What does he need to decide for himself?

Solicit brief responses from the group.

5 minutes

ON YOUR OWN: What You Expect from Friends

Please turn to page 56 in your Participant's Guide.

Each one of us has different expectations of our friends. The following 5-minute exercise will help us clarify what we expect from our closest friends.

Read each statement and circle T (true) or F (false) for each one. Be as honest as you can.

After 4 minutes have gone by, warn the group that they have 1 minute remaining to complete the exercise. Conclude the first exercise after 5 minutes have elapsed.

Video: What to Do When Friends Fail

Anne's Phone Conversation with Mark

Why Friends Fail: Change, Neglect, Betrayal

Five Steps to Reclaiming a Friendship

- Count the cost.
- Make meaningful contact.
- Forgive as best you can.
- Diagnose the problem.
- Rebuild respect.

On Your Own: What You Expect from Friends

This exercise will help you clarify what you expect from your closest friends. Answer the following true-or-false statements as honestly as you can.

T F I expect my friend to know my faults but accept me anyway.
T F I expect my friend to never break special plans with me.
T F I expect my close friends to always keep their word on both big and small issues.
T F A really good friend should know how I'm feeling most of the time.
T F I expect my friend to say "I'm sorry" when he or she is wrong.
T F My closest friend should confide in me more than anyone else.
T F I expect my friend to always keep a secret.
T F It is difficult for me to forgive a friend who has hurt me in some way.
T F If we are truly friends, we should hardly ever have much conflict.
T F I expect my friends to never talk behind my back or break a confidence—even about small things.
T F My very closest friend should have no other friendships closer than ours.
T F If a good friend breaks a confidence or fails me in some other way, I am unlikely to give him or her a second or third chance.
T F I expect my friend to never hold a grudge against me.
T F I expect my friend to always admit when he or she is wrong.

If you answered true to any of these items, you are more likely to have very high standards about how your friends should treat you. The more times you answered true, the more you expect from your friends and perhaps the more rigid you are with your expectations.

5 minutes

CONFERENCE CALL: Why Do Some Friends Fail?

Turn to page 58 in the Participant's Guide. Let's take the next 5 minutes to discuss failed friendships. Why do some friends fail?

> Possible answers include: *change* (move away, marriage, change in job), *neglect* (just don't have time to communicate), and *betrayal.* Allow a minute or two to discuss this first question.

Have any of you ever had a friendship that failed? Perhaps one from your childhood. Briefly explain what happened and what your expectations were for this friendship.

> Be prepared to share a story from your own experience to get the ball rolling.

9 minutes

ON YOUR OWN: Learning from Your Own Failed Relationships

Please turn to page 59 in your Participant's Guide.

This exercise is designed to help us gain insights into how we can avoid repeating patterns of painful relationships. Take 9 minutes to consider a relationship where a person you trusted failed you in some way. Write your answers to the questions in the spaces provided.

> After 8 minutes, give the class a 1-minute warning. Conclude the exercise after 9 minutes.

Conference Call: Why Do Some Friends Fail?

- Why do friends fail?
- What friendships have failed for you? What happened? What were your expectations for these friendships?

On Your Own: Learning from Your Own Failed Friendships

This exercise is designed to help you gain insight into how you can avoid repeating patterns of painful relationships. Consider a relationship where a person you trusted failed you in some way, and answer the following questions to help you learn from the failure.

1. How long did you know this person, and what brought you together?

2. Looking back over your relationship, what kinds of things helped you to believe you could trust him or her?

3. In specific terms, what did this person do to "fail" you?

4. What percentage of the hurt was due to the following:

   Percentage
   ____ miscommunication
   ____ broken confidence
   ____ gossip
   ____ neglect
   ____ betrayal
   ____ uncontrollable change (moving away)
   ____ personality change
   ____ moral choices
   ____ other ____________________

5. Do some serious soul-searching and try to assess how much you were responsible for the falling-out with this friend. Was there anything you did or didn't do that may have contributed to the problem? If so, what was it?

6. Did you ever want to get revenge as a result of the hurt you felt from this relationship? If so, why? Also, what did you do with your vengeful feelings, and what was the result?

7. Have you come to a place of healing with the hurt you experienced? If so, what helped bring this about?

8. In reviewing the basis for your relationship and the reasons for your falling-out, what can you surmise about how to avoid a similar situation in future friendships?

5 minutes

HUDDLE TIME: The Hurt Involved in Failed Relationships

Break up into small groups of three to four people, then turn to page 61 of your Participant's Guide.

Note the questions listed there. Take about 5 minutes to discuss these questions among yourselves.

After 4 minutes, give the class a 1-minute warning to wrap up their small-group discussions. Conclude the discussion after 5 minutes.

10 minutes

CONFERENCE CALL: Five Steps in Restoring Failed Relationships

So far we've talked about why and how relationships fail—some of the main reasons and the feelings that go along with losing a friend. Now we're going to examine five steps we can take to restore failed relationships.

Please turn to page 62 in your Participant's Guide.

Let's take a few moments to fill in the blanks at the top of your page.

There are five steps to take in restoring a broken relationship:

- *Step One: Count the cost.* DETERMINE whether your fractured friendship should be REPAIRED.
- *Step Two: Make meaningful contact.* Keep the message SIMPLE. Convey your desire to resolve your differences and explore their openness to considering a DISCUSSION.
- *Step Three: Forgive as best you can.* Our primal urge for BALANCING THE SCORE comes to a screeching halt when we set our PRIDE aside and begin to FORGIVE.
- *Step Four: Diagnose the problem.* Acknowledge the PROBLEM. Realize that everyone is partially GOOD and partially BAD.
- *Step Five: Rebuild respect.* Begin by noting your friend's most ADMIRABLE QUALITIES. Next, own up to your mistakes. Offer a SINCERE APOLOGY.

Of all the steps listed, which one do you think would be the most difficult to take? What stumbling blocks might get in the way of making meaningful contact or forgiving the other person or diagnosing the problem or even rebuilding respect?

Solicit brief responses from the group.

Huddle Time: The Hurt Involved in Failed Friendships

- What caused the most hurt for you in a failed relationship you experienced?
- In what ways have you overcome the hurt you felt? Have you resolved those hurt feelings?

Conference Call: Five Steps in Restoring Failed Relationships

There are five steps to take in restoring a broken relationship:

- *Step One: Count the cost.* ____________________ whether your fractured friendship should be ________________.
- *Step Two: Make meaningful contact.* Keep the message ______________. Convey your desire to resolve your differences and explore their openness to considering a ________________________.
- *Step Three: Forgive as best you can.* Our primal urge for ____________________________ comes to a screeching halt when we set our ______________ aside and begin to ____________________.
- *Step Four: Diagnose the problem.* Acknowledge the __________________. Realize that everyone is partially __________ and partially __________.
- *Step Five: Rebuild respect.* Begin by noting your friend's most ____________________________. Next, own up to your mistakes. Offer a __________________________.

Of all the steps listed above, which one do you think would be the most difficult to take? What stumbling blocks might get in the way of making meaningful contact, forgiving the other person, diagnosing the problem, or even rebuilding respect?

planning notes

2 minutes

SESSION SUMMARY

We covered a lot of information during this session. We looked at friendships that fail and explored how much we can expect from a friend. We examined why and how friends fail, then we discussed five steps we can take to reconcile a failed or damaged relationship.

Please turn to page 63 in your Participant's Guide.

This week's Extra-Mile Exercise is for those of us who have a failed or strained relationship we would like to see restored. Following through on the five steps in this exercise will help us build the bridge that can lead to reconciliation.

1 minute

CLOSING PRAYER

Lord, help us to place our failed relationships in your hands. If there is a relationship that can be restored, give us the courage and commitment to take the steps necessary to begin the process. Please work in our friends' lives and hearts too, so they will be receptive to our efforts. In Jesus' name, amen.

Extra-Mile Exercise

Making amends can be the most difficult task in any relationship. Often there is a battle between our head and our heart. Our head wants to stay angry, to recount the wrongs we've endured; but our heart yearns to recapture the joy we once felt with that friend. Consider following these guidelines to help you bring healing and restoration to a floundering relationship.

Step One: Count the Cost

What is the price you are paying to keep this friendship alive? If you were forced to choose between the following two statements, which one would best describe how you feel about this relationship?

1. This relationship has redeeming qualities I value, and it is worth the cost of repairing and maintaining.
2. This relationship is unhealthy and forces me to compromise my convictions.

If you chose the second statement, it is time to make a clean break. If you chose the first statement, you are ready to make amends by progressing to the next step.

Step Two: Make Meaningful Contact

What will be the best way for you to let your friend know that the friendship is valuable to you and that you want to restore it? Knowing your friend, should you initiate contact through a brief note, a phone call, or a visit?

Once you determine the means, take care to send the right message by cleaning your heart and mind of lingering desires to get back at your friend. Take a moment right now to note what has hurt you and how you may still want to get even. Be honest with yourself about your anger and feelings of revenge.

Step Three: Forgive as Best You Can

Once you have a handle on your hurt and angry feelings, you will need to do your best to step beyond them by trying to forgive. While not easy, it is vital if you are going to make amends. Put yourself in your friend's shoes and try to see the relationship and situation from his or her perspective.

1. How do you imagine your friend feels about what is going on between the two of you?
2. Is your friend feeling as hurt as you are? If you think so, why?
3. If the roles were reversed, how do you think the relationship would be different?
4. Knowing that hardly any relationship problem is ever entirely one person's fault, what responsibility do you take for this situation?
5. Are you able and willing to set aside your pride and give grace to your friend? If so, how can you do this?

Step Four: Diagnose the Problem

Once you have come to a place where you can forgive your friend and convey the simple message of wanting to make things right, the two of you may need to explore together why the problem emerged so that it won't happen again. It's up to the two of you to determine

whether this step of having an honest discussion of differences is necessary.

Step Five: Rebuild Respect

This last step is critical to making amends. Ask yourself what traits your friend possesses that inspire you to become a better person, and then make a list of a half dozen of your friend's most admirable qualities.

1.
2.
3.
4.
5.
6.

With this list completed, you are now ready to make amends. You will be able to express to your friend just how much you appreciate him or her based on these qualities.

Session Six

relating to God without feeling phony

BEFORE YOU LEAD

Synopsis

I (Les) was brought up in a religious home—a parsonage, no less—and I make no bones about it. I inherited my faith in God about the time I was old enough to eat graham crackers.

As a child I didn't weigh the evidence for accepting or rejecting religious beliefs. In fact, I didn't even know there were options.

In college I learned to evaluate and question. As a college sophomore, sitting in the cafeteria, I suddenly saw my routine of saying the blessing at meals in a new light. The whole thing seemed perfunctory, a meaningless ritual. I wondered why I prayed.

I'm not sure how long I suffered in the darkness of doubt, but somewhere in the midst of my lonely questioning I realized something that eventually revolutionized my faith: I was not searching for an explanation. I was longing for a relationship.

Finding God

Doubt dismantled the faith of my childhood. And I thank God for doubt. It gave me faith—a faith of my own. I have come to understand what Tennyson meant when he said, "There lies more faith in honest doubt than in all your creeds."

If you want to relate to God without feeling phony, therefore, you've got to fess up. You've got to admit your doubts, ask your questions, and start getting real with God.

Who Is God?

According to a contemporary parable, a group of scientists was recently commissioned to build a computer that could answer with scientific precision the question of God's existence. After completing the most intricate, sophisticated computer ever assembled, the scientists carefully fed the question into their machine: "Is there a God?" After several minutes of humming and whirring, the answer came out. It read: "There is now."

Sigmund Freud, founder of modern psychology, proposed that God is nothing more than the imaginary projection of the father figure. Emile Durkheim, one of the founders of modern sociology, viewed God as nothing more than a symbolic representation of the collective values of society.

What do you think? Rather than viewing Freud and Durkheim's theories as negating the possibility of believing in a transcendent, eternal God, do they not simply explain the origin of false deities against which we must struggle? Consider the following distorted concepts of God.

- *The Referee God.* Some people see God as a referee who tallies points for good performance on a huge scoreboard in the sky. These people are consumed by religious rules and the fear that they will step out of line and suffer a penalty.
- *The Grandfather God.* Many people use their interpretation of God to keep them from growing up—to avoid responsibility. They want to be told, "There is nothing to worry about; I'll take care of everything for you."
- *The Scientist God.* "A superior reasoning power," is how Einstein conceptualized God. For some, God is a withdrawn and distant thinker, too busy running the galaxies to get involved in our petty problems.
- *The Bodyguard God.* Some people think of God much the same way a sailor thinks of a lifeboat. He knows it is there, but he hopes he'll never have to use it. These people live life without giving much conscious attention to God, but they expect him to be there when they need him.

Countless volumes over the centuries have been written by philosophers and theologians on the attributes of God. And we are not so naïve as to think we can sum up God's character in a few paragraphs of this chapter. So permit us to lift out of Scripture God's cardinal trait, the one quality that describes who God is more than any other: God is love.

Who Needs God?

In the first chapter of this book we explored the "compulsion for completion" that every person brings to an important relationship. And we discovered that this compulsion can never be fulfilled at the human level.

God is love. And here is a relational principle that is more powerful than dynamite: We cannot love until we first experience love. The more love we experience in our critical early years, the more mature and healthy our love for others will be as adults. It's a universal tenet. And it's grounded in our innate need for God.

How Do You Relate to God?

Let's cut to it. If you want to relate to God without feeling phony, you've got to get rid of everything that distorts, dilutes, or compromises the person you were meant to be, until only your authentic self—created in God's image—remains. The bottom line? You've got to get real. Be honest. The more you can admit who you are—even when you wish you were different—the deeper your relationship with God will grow.

Once you come to God as a real person, you are ready to build a relationship like any other. But God is invisible, you say, and mysterious. True. But God also provided us with a flesh-and-blood connection to himself through Jesus Christ. In human flesh, Jesus experienced a range of emotions: playfulness with children, sympathy for the sick, joy with his disciples, anger at legalists, grief for the brokenhearted, loneliness and anguish in Gethsemane and on the cross. Jesus was God in human form. So when you consider how you might relate to an "invisible" God without feeling phony, consider how you might relate to Jesus.

But be forewarned: "No one who meets Jesus ever stays the same." So writes Philip Yancey in his wonderful book *The Jesus I Never Knew*.

Session Sequence (50 minutes total)

Welcome (1 minute)
Opening Prayer (1 minute)
Review and Overview (2 minutes)
Video (6 minutes)
On Your Own (10 minutes)
Huddle Time (8 minutes)
Conference Call (5 minutes)
On Your Own (8 minutes)
Huddle Time (6 minutes)
Session Summary (2 minutes)
Closing Prayer (1 minute)

Session Six

relating to God without feeling phony

1 minute

WELCOME

Call the group together. Welcome the participants to Session 6 of *Relationships*: "Relating to God Without Feeling Phony."

1 minute

OPENING PRAYER

Dear Father, as we conclude this series on relationships, we want to focus on the most important relationship we can have—the one we have with you. Even though we disappoint you at times and even though we have our doubts, we are grateful that you are faithful and forgiving. Help us to strengthen our relationship with you through your Son, Jesus Christ. In Jesus' name, amen.

2 minutes

REVIEW AND OVERVIEW

During Session 5 we took a look at failed friendships. We explored how much we can expect from our friends, and how many demands we make on our friends, both implicit and explicit. We also examined why and how friends fail, and we learned that there are three "friendship killers"—change, neglect, and betrayal. Finally, we looked at five steps we can take toward reconciling damaged or failed relationships.

Turn to page 68 in your Participant's Guide for our session overview.

In this final session, we're going to examine the most important relationship we can ever have—the one we have with God. We will discuss our doubts and fears. Is it okay to doubt? Then we will discover how to really relate to God. And finally, we will hear about some different conceptions of God.

Session Six

relating to God
without feeling phony

Overview

In this session you will

- discuss your doubts and fears. Is it okay to doubt?
- discover how to really relate to God.
- hear some different conceptions of God.

planning notes

6 minutes

VIDEO: Relating to God Without Feeling Phony

The previous video segments have dealt with various relationships: Now we're going to deal with the most important relationship of all. And, as we'll see, our relationship with God can actually be a great influence on our earthly relationships. All of us wrestle with doubt occasionally, and Les and Leslie Parrott will give us some guidelines to use when we face our own doubts.

There is space provided for taking notes on page 69 in your Participant's Guide.

Start the video; turn it off at the prompt.

10 minutes

ON YOUR OWN: Honest-to-Goodness Doubt

Please turn to page 70 in your Participant's Guide.

Contained in this exercise are some questions for you to consider: (1) What is your experience with doubt? (2) Does your doubt impact your relationship with God? (3) Do you bury your doubt in an attempt to pretend that everything about your faith is fine?

We're going to take the next 10 minutes to complete an exercise designed to help us consider our faith and the degree to which we struggle with doubts. The continuum will help you consider your level of faith. For example, if you circle number 1 for the for the first set of statements, you are saying you have no faith at all; if you circle a number in the middle, you're saying your faith is somewhere between nonexistent and rock solid. Circle a number for each set of statements that best describes you. When you are done, look back over your responses. Write a single-sentence summary of your level of faith or doubt.

Any questions?

After 9 minutes have gone by, warn the group that they have 1 minute remaining to complete the exercise. Conclude the exercise after 10 minutes have elapsed.

Video: Relating to God Without Feeling Phony

Relating to God Relaxes Our Earthly Relationships

Curing Our Compulsion for Completion—Anne's Example

Doubt as Normal—Do I Have a Relationship with God?

Various Misconceptions of God—Referee, Grandfather, Scientist, Bodyguard

God as the Antidote for the Compulsion for Completion

On Your Own: Honest-to-Goodness Doubt

How much do you struggle with doubt? The following continuums will help you consider your level of faith. Be as honest as you can in your responses.

My "faith" is nonexistent. — My faith is rock solid.

1 2 3 4 5 6 7 8 9 10

I don't know God. — I know God personally.

1 2 3 4 5 6 7 8 9 10

The Bible is just another book. — The Bible is a holy book inspired by God.

1 2 3 4 5 6 7 8 9 10

Jesus was simply an historical figure. — Jesus is my personal Savior.

1 2 3 4 5 6 7 8 9 10

God doesn't hear my prayers. — God hears and answers my prayers.

1 2 3 4 5 6 7 8 9 10

As you consider where you stand on the above continuums, take a moment to summarize your faith in a single sentence.

____

____

Now take a moment to summarize your doubt in a single sentence.

____

____

planning notes

8 minutes

HUDDLE TIME: Doubt's Place in Building Faith

Please break into small groups of three or four, then turn to page 71 in your Participant's Guide.

In the light of the exercise we've just completed, take about 8 minutes to discuss the following questions: (1) Does doubt have any place in an authentic relationship with God? Why or why not? (2) Do you believe God can help a person find a faith of his or her own? Explain.

After 7 minutes have gone by, give your group the 1-minute warning. Stop the discussion after 8 minutes have elapsed.

5 minutes

CONFERENCE CALL: Misperceptions of God

Please turn to page 72 in your Participant's Guide.

In the video, we saw a few misperceptions people often have about who God is. Do you identify with any of these? If so, in what way? If not, what misperception of God's character have you experienced?

If the group has a difficult time starting out, you may want to rephrase the question. Ask how they viewed God when they were children. Conclude the discussion after 5 minutes have elapsed.

8 minutes

ON YOUR OWN: Does God Really Love Me?

Please turn to page 73 in your Participant's Guide.

This exercise will help us assess the degree to which we experience God's love on a personal level. Rate each statement on page 73, using the scale near the top of the page, to indicate how often each statement represents your beliefs. We'll take about 8 minutes to complete this exercise.

After 7 minutes, give the class a 1-minute warning to wrap up the exercise. Conclude the exercise after 8 minutes.

Huddle Time: Doubt's Place in Building Faith

In light of the exercise you just completed, discuss the following:

1. Does doubt have any place in an authentic relationship with God? Why or why not?
2. Do you believe God can help a person find a faith of his or her own? Explain.

Conference Call: Misperceptions of God

- In the video, Leslie mentioned a few misperceptions people have about who God is. Do you identify with any of these? If so, how?

- If not, what misperception of God's character have you experienced?

On Your Own: Does God Really Love Me?

This exercise is designed to help you assess the degree to which you experience God's love on a personal level. Rate each statement, using the scale below, to indicate how often each represents your beliefs. Take your time and be as honest as you can.

1—Rarely or never
2—A little of the time
3—Some of the time
4—A good part of the time
5—Most or all of the time

____ I believe nothing could ever separate me from God's love.
____ I accept how special I am to God.
____ I believe God is love.
____ God's grace permeates my life.
____ I'm confident that because God loves me so much, he sacrificed his only Son in my place.
____ I believe God loves me as if I were the only person on earth.
____ I am free from irrational guilt feelings because of God's love.
____ I believe I can do nothing to earn God's love because it's freely given.
____ I know God loves me.
____ I can love others because God first loved me.

Total score _______ x 2 = ________

Scoring: Add up your item scores and multiply your total by two. This provides a possible maximum score of 100. Use the following to interpret your score:

90–100 You have a solid and secure understanding of how much God loves you.

80–89 You may experience some ambivalence at times about how much God loves you, but deep down you rest in knowing that he does love you.

10–79 You are struggling to know whether God loves you or not. If your score is below 60, you would certainly benefit from counsel on God's grace.

6 minutes

HUDDLE TIME: Why We Need God

Please break up into small groups of three or four people, then turn to page 75 in your Participant's Guide.

Take the next 6 minutes to discuss the question: If someone were to ask you why a person needs God, what would your answer be?

After 5 minutes have gone by, give the class a 1-minute warning. Stop the discussion after 6 minutes have elapsed.

2 minute

SESSION SUMMARY

In our final session together, we examined the most important relationship we can ever have—the one we have with God. We discussed our doubts and fears and whether it is okay to doubt. Then we discovered how to really relate to God.

Please turn to page 76 in your Participant's Guide.

Our final Extra-Mile Exercise may seem simple, but it is probably the most difficult one of all. It is designed to help you see how you presently relate to God and how you want to relate to him in the future. This can be a valuable tool to help you formulate the steps you'll need to take in order to develop your relationship with him.

1 minute

CLOSING PRAYER

Lord, during this course we have learned about developing healthy relationships—starting with becoming healthier ourselves. We've examined how our families of origin affect every relationship we have. We've explored the ways you have made men and women different from each other, and we have tried to gain a better appreciation for each other's qualities. We've also investigated the intricacies of friendship—what constitutes a "good" friend and what causes friendships to fail. Through all of these important relationships, we ask that you guide and lead us. And that brings us to the most important relationship any of us could ever have—the one we share individually with you. Help us, Lord, to continually grow and nurture our relationship with you. In Jesus' name, amen.

Huddle Time: Why We Need God

- If someone were to ask you why a person needs God, what would your answer be?

Extra-Mile Exercise

This final exercise may seem simple, but it is probably the most difficult one of all. It is designed to help you see how you relate to God now and how you want to relate to God in the future. It will help you formulate the steps necessary to develop your relationship with him.

In a single sentence, summarize your faith journey and how it has brought you to your present relationship with God. Then note a few key descriptors of your present relationship with him.

Take a moment to consider how you might represent your present relationship with God by drawing a picture of it. Be as creative as you like. Use a separate piece of paper, if you wish.

Once you have completed your drawing, consider which aspects you would like to change to make it more like the relationship you long for. What would those changes involve?

What can you do, in practical terms, to make that kind of relationship with God a reality?

planning notes

Exciting Marriage Preparation for Today's Young Couples

Saving Your Marriage Before It Starts

Seven Questions to Ask Before (And After) You Marry

Drs. Les & Leslie Parrott

Did you know many couples spend more time preparing for their wedding than they do for their marriage?

Having tasted firsthand the difficulties of "wedding bell blues," Drs. Les and Leslie Parrott show young couples the skills they need to make the transition from "single" to "married" smooth and enjoyable.

Saving Your Marriage Before It Starts is more than a book—it's practically a premarital counseling session. A few questions that will be explored are:

- Question 1: Have You Faced the Myths of Marriage with Honesty?
- Question 3: Have You Developed the Habit of Happiness?
- Question 6: Do You Know How to Fight a Good Fight?

Questions at the end of every chapter help you explore each topic personally. Companion men's and women's workbooks full of self-tests and exercises will help you apply what you learn. And the *Saving Your Marriage Before It Starts* video curriculum will help you learn and grow with other couples who are dealing with the same struggles and questions.

Here's what the experts are saying about *Saving Your Marriage Before It Starts:*

> *"I've spent the past twenty-five years developing material to strengthen marriages. I wish* Saving Your Marriage Before It Starts *had been developed years ago."*
>
> —H. Norman Wright, Author of *Before You Say I Do*

> *"The Parrotts have a unique way of capturing fresh insights from research and then showing the practical implications from personal experience. This is one of the few 'must read' books on marriage."*
>
> —Dr. David Stoop, Clinical Psychologist, Cohost of the New Life Clinics Radio Program

WINNER OF THE 1996 ECPA GOLD MEDALLION BOOK AWARDS

Hardcover 0-310-49240-8
Audio Pages 0-310-49248-3
Video Curriculum 0-310-20451-8
Workbook for Men 0-310-48731-5
Workbook for Women 0-310-48741-2

Becoming Soul Mates

52 Meditations to Bring Joy to Your Marriage

Les & Leslie Parrott

Becoming Soul Mates gives you a road map for cultivating rich spiritual intimacy in your relationship. Fifty-two practical weekly devotions help you and your partner dig deep for a strong spiritual foundation in the early years of marriage.

In each session you will find:

- An insightful devotion that focuses on marriage-related topics
- A key passage of Scripture
- Questions that will spark discussions on crucial issues
- Insights from real-life soul mates like Pat and Shirley Boone, Bill and Vonette Bright, and Norm and Joyce Wright
- Questions that will help you and your partner better understand each other's unique needs and remember them in prayer during the week.

Start building on the closeness you've got today and reap the rewards of a deep, more satisfying relationship in the years ahead. Pick up *Becoming Soul Mates* at your local Christian bookstore.

Hardcover 0-310-20014-8

Questions Couples Ask

Answers to the Top 100 Marital Questions

Dr. Les Parrott III & Dr. Leslie Parrott

Ask yourself the following.....

- How can I be honest without hurting my partner's feelings?
- What do we do when one of us is a spender and one of us is a hoarder?
- What can we do to protect our marriage against extramarital affairs?
- How can we be more spiritually intimate as a married couple?

From communication, conflict, and careers to sex, in-laws, and money, *Questions Couples Ask* is your first stop for help with the foremost hurdles of marriage. Drs. Les and Leslie Parrott share cutting-edge insights for the 100 top questions married couples ask. Whether you want to improve your own marriage or nurture the marriages of others, Christianity's premier husband-wife marriage counseling team equips you with expert advice for building a thriving relationship.

> *"Today's married couples find it hard to get the answers they need to their marital questions. They're often so overwhelmed that they don't even know what questions to ask. Les and Leslie Parrott give us the right questions to be thinking about—and the right answers."*
>
> —Dr. Robert G. Barnes,
> Sheridan House Family Ministries

To find answers to these and many other marital questions, pick up your copy of *Questions Couples Ask* at a Christian bookstore near you.

Softcover 0-310-20754-1

ZondervanPublishingHouse
Grand Rapids, Michigan
http://www.zondervan.com

Love
is . . .
Meditations for Couples
on 1 Corinthians 13
Les & Leslie Parrott

Like a Kiss on the Lips

Devotions from Proverbs for Couples

Les Parrott & Leslie Parrott

"An honest answer is like a kiss on the lips."
—Proverbs 24:26

Drs. Les and Leslie Parrott know that wisdom is the bedrock of a healthy marriage. Great marriages are shaped by wise principles—principles set forth centuries ago by Israel's wisest king, Solomon.

This book takes couples to the book of Proverbs for insights that can help build and fortify a relationship. Thirty-one devotionals explore key verses and colorful anecdotes from the Parrotts' life experience that touch on every aspect of marriage:

- communication
- money
- sex
- commitment
- anger
- forgiveness
- praise
- humility
- conflict
- and more!

The wise saying of Proverbs must be talked about, say the Parrotts. "Read them aloud together. Commit a few to memory. And fill your marriage with wise and good conversation."

Pick up your copy of *Like a Kiss on the Lips* at your local Christian bookstore.

Hardcover 0-310-21623-0

ZondervanPublishingHouse
Grand Rapids, Michigan
http://www.zondervan.com

We want to hear from you. Please send your comments about this book to us in care of the address below. Thank you.

ZondervanPublishingHouse
Grand Rapids, Michigan 49530
http://www.zondervan.com